Winston Churchill by his Personal Secretary

The author, from a photograph taken during the war.

Winston Churchill by his Personal Secretary

◆

Recollections of The Great Man by A Woman Who Worked for Him

throughout the crucial war years from 1941 to 1945

Elizabeth Nel

iUniverse, Inc.
New York Lincoln Shanghai

Winston Churchill by his Personal Secretary
Recollections of The Great Man by A Woman Who Worked for Him

Copyright © 2007, 2008 by Elizabeth Nel

All rights reserved. No part of this book may be used or reproduced by any means, graphic, electronic, or mechanical, including photocopying, recording, taping or by any information storage retrieval system without the written permission of the publisher except in the case of brief quotations embodied in critical articles and reviews.

iUniverse books may be ordered through booksellers or by contacting:

iUniverse
2021 Pine Lake Road, Suite 100
Lincoln, NE 68512
www.iuniverse.com
1-800-Authors (1-800-288-4677)

Because of the dynamic nature of the Internet, any Web addresses or links contained in this book may have changed since publication and may no longer be valid.

The views expressed in this work are solely those of the author and do not necessarily reflect the views of the publisher, and the publisher hereby disclaims any responsibility for them.

Originally published under the title *Mr. Churchill's Secretary* by Hodder and Stoughton in 1958.

ISBN: 978-0-595-46852-2 (pbk)
ISBN: 978-0-595-91144-8 (ebk)

Printed in the United States of America

To

ANDREA, DEBORAH and FRANÇOIS,

for whose sake this book was written

Do not let us speak of darker days: let us speak rather of sterner days. These are not dark days; these are great days—the greatest days our country has ever lived; and we must all thank God that we have been allowed, each of us according to our stations, to play a part in making these days memorable in the history of our race.
—Winston Churchill, address to Harrow School, 1941

Contents

List of Illustrations xi
Editor's Note xiii
Foreword. xv
Introduction xix
CHAPTER 1 1
CHAPTER 2 6
CHAPTER 3 13
CHAPTER 4 18
CHAPTER 5 25
CHAPTER 6 34
CHAPTER 7 42
CHAPTER 8 49
CHAPTER 9 56
CHAPTER 10 65
CHAPTER 11. 72
CHAPTER 12 80
CHAPTER 13 85
CHAPTER 14 92
CHAPTER 15 99

CHAPTER 16 107
CHAPTER 17 116
CHAPTER 18 124
CHAPTER 19 130
CHAPTER 20 136
Afterword 139
Epilogue 143
APPENDIX 1 Recollections by Elizabeth Nel's children 149
APPENDIX 2 *Elizabeth Nel:* Obituary by David Twiston 153

List of Illustrations

The author, from a photograph taken during the war . . . . *ii*

The signed portrait of Churchill which he gave to the author *63*

The Hawtrey Room at Chequers in which the Prime Minister often used to dictate. *64*

The author at her desk at Chequers. *114*

The author and Marion with officers aboard H.M.S. Ajax. *115*

The author in 1958 with her husband, Frans, François 2, Deborah 7, Andrea 11. . . . . *122*

Mr. Churchill at the end of his V.E. broadcast. *123*

Elizabeth Nel at home in 2007 . . . . *141*

Editor's Note

It is with great sadness that I heard that Elizabeth Nel, the author of this book, had passed away at her home in South Africa on October 30th 2007, by which time the Foreword, which follows, had already been written. In fact, a number of early release copies of this book had been printed prior to her death, and it is comforting to know that Elizabeth had the joy of receiving and reading her newly updated book. Her friends, the Rev Duncan Murray and Celia Murray, who visited her on 14th October, were pleased that, although frail, Elizabeth was delighted with the book. In a sense, she had seen that her work had, in the words of her son François, "completed a full circle".

I am indebted to David Twiston, Chief Obituary Editor of the *Daily Telegraph*, for his kind permission to reproduce his excellent obituary of Elizabeth Nel as an Appendix in this edition.

Thanks are also due to Phil Reed, Director of the Churchill Museum at the Cabinet War Rooms, for so kindly offering to make the premises available for the book launch. The author was closely connected with the Museum and is fondly remembered by both Phil Reed and his Personal Secretary, Joanne Grenier-Morton, to whom I am also grateful for providing some additional information and for drawing my attention to some inaccuracies that have now been corrected.

Charles Muller
December 2007

Foreword

It was at a book launch in Kelso, in the Scottish Borders, where I met the Rev. Duncan Murray and his wife, Celia, who drew my attention to Elizabeth Nel and her book on Winston Churchill. Duncan, with Celia, had recently left South Africa to settle in Scotland, in order to take up a call in the Church of Scotland, and had been close friends of Elizabeth, in South Africa, for many years.

I wrote to Elizabeth Nel and received a glowing letter in reply—yes, she would be very agreeable to a new edition of her book, the original for many years now being out of print. Having read through her account of her experiences working for Winston Churchill, I was so intrigued, not only by her portrayal of that irascible yet loveable hero of World War II, but by her own charming personality that shines through every line of her captivating style, that I found I wanted to know more about her—about what happened to her, or what she did, after she left her life at No.10 and moved to South Africa—and surely any reader today would be equally eager to know how her life continued over the past sixty years. I suggested this to Duncan and Celia, and Celia was kind enough to phone her friend Lionel Heath, who lives in Port Elizabeth, not far from Elizabeth Nel, asking him if he would act as her scribe for an additional chapter, or an updated piece that might be included at the end of this volume. Elizabeth Nel had just turned 90, and Celia thought this would be a less strenuous burden for Elizabeth than that involved in writing the piece herself. Lionel Heath was agreeable to this, and so his valuable contribution has been included in this volume as an Epilogue. (As it happens, I did in fact receive an enlightening contribution from Elizabeth Nel herself, just in time, when I had already received the first proofs of this edition, and it gives me great pleasure to include this piece as an Afterword, immediately following her original text. Her contribution shows that, even at 90, her memories are as crisp, and her mind as incisive, as ever! And a further happy development—Celia later thought I might approach Elizabeth's three children in South Africa, asking them if they, too, would like a final say in the book, describing what it was like to grow up with a mother who had been Winston Churchill's personal secretary. That piece, too, arrived just in time, at the proof stage, and has been added to this volume as an Appendix. My sincere thanks are due to Andrea, the eldest of the three children, for her help in liaising with her brother François, and sister Deborah, and to all three of them for their combined efforts in writing this valuable additional piece with its new insights.)

Celia's mother Jean van't Hoogerhuijs was Elizabeth's closest and dearest friend, so Celia recalls with warmth and admiration so much of what Jean and Elizabeth strove for through the National Council of Women and the Collegiate School for Girls school committee (on which she served from 1962-1975); therefore Celia herself has been able to provide some updated information about this remarkable lady who has been engaged in many talks about Winston Churchill. Celia pointed out that Elizabeth Nel's daughters, Andrea and Debbie, are Old Girls of the Collegiate School for Girls in Port Elizabeth, Elizabeth herself being a very special Honorary Member of the Old Collegiate Girl's Guild; and she very kindly sent me the following article written by Elizabeth Nel about the time she met the Queen (on 7th February 2005) when she visited London to be at the opening of the Churchill Museum, an article that appeared in the *Old Collegiate Girl's Guild* newsletter:

AN EPIC JOURNEY—by Elizabeth Nel

On 7th February, 2005, my daughter and I flew to London, I having been invited (instructed!) to attend the official opening of the Churchill Museum by Her Majesty the Queen. We were taken at once by taxi-car to the Churchill Hotel, and having settled in we were fetched by an official cab and taken to the Cabinet War Rooms, where the Museum is situated—not far from Big Ben and the House of Parliament, equally near to No.10, under a huge concrete block which was constructed at ground level, at the beginning of the war, to shelter the precious place in case of bombs falling. In war days I worked and slept there on a regular basis.

We had a quick look around the Museum. The first thing I saw, in a place of honour, was "my" cigar, retrieved from the fireplace where Mr. Churchill had thrown it, after only a few puffs, and kept by me, in care and safety, for almost 60 years. This was a few days before the end of the war in Europe.

Next day there was a big press conference which I had to attend, being almost the only member of his personal staff still living. They were all very kind and appreciative. It was indeed a long journey to make.

Then it was the 10th, the Big Day. We were all placed ready for Her Majesty, who was to name and open the Museum. I was in the place of Honour, to be introduced first, and as she approached I could see she was looking tense and upset; Charles and Camilla had that morning announced their plans to wed. After greeting us all individually, The Queen made a charming short speech, ending with the naming of the Churchill Museum and pronouncing it now open. She then retired, and others of her party, notably the Duke of Kent and Mrs. Thatcher, came to speak to us also. There was a delightful finger lunch, then Debs and I went off for a very little treat—we stayed the night with Celia Sandys, grand-daughter of the Churchills, and her dear family, at their lovely home just near Marlborough in Wiltshire.

Elizabeth Nel was a strong member of The National Council of Women; in fact, she was given an honorary life vice-presidency. She shared these interests with Celia's mother who was her special friend and colleague until her death in 2003. In fact, Celia recalls, Elizabeth sat beside her at her mother's funeral and gave her hand a knowing squeeze at appropriate moments—something Celia says she will never forget.

Celia went on to say that Elizabeth Nel is "certainly the most charming, intelligent, caring, outgoing, confident lady who communicates very well and can move up and down the social order with ease. She is an extrovert—who has always carried out her convictions with courage and determination, especially when it was for the needs of others."

Today Elizabeth Nel lives in her home in Sunridge Park, which is filled with furniture made and turned by her late husband, Frans Nel. The furniture items are beautifully made out of South African wood, such as Kiaat and Stinkwood. Elizabeth is very proud of them, Celia says, and rightly so. Frans was a very special man, to be married to someone like Elizabeth. He had a wonderful sense of humour and he was a very gracious host.

The above, Celia said, are "just a few thoughts on a wonderful friend who has been an inspiration to so many." She and Duncan will be taking her out to dinner on their next visit to South Africa, in October, 2007, and have had to book the date in Elizabeth's diary—"can you beat it," Celia says, "at 90 years of age!" Hopefully this new edition will be ready by the time they go to South Africa, for they plan to take copies of the book with them to present personally to Elizabeth Nel.

My sincere thanks are due to both Duncan and Celia Murray for drawing my attention to Elizabeth Nel, as well as to Lionel Heath who so kindly interviewed her (and photographed her!) and who so meticulously jotted down her thoughts as well as his own impressions of this very elegant and remarkable personal secretary to whom, in a very real sense, we all owe a great debt for the vital role she played in helping that bulldog of a man, Winston Churchill, win the Second World War for the sake of freedom and justice.

Charles Muller
MA (Wales), PhD (Lond.), D.Litt (OFS), D.Ed (SA)
DIADEM BOOKS
www.diadembooks.com

Introduction

It doesn't really matter who I am or where I came from. Without undue modesty, the only thing of real interest about me is that during World War II I worked for four and a half years as one of the Personal Secretaries to Sir Winston Churchill. Much time has passed since those days: I have not seen him for nearly thirteen years.[1] All that time I have felt a desire to write about him, *the* man, the outstanding figure of our time, and the years I spent in his service. I have had much to learn here, in South Africa, and some difficulties to overcome. But now I have a little more time; the children have all arrived, and housekeeping is less of a mystery. Therefore I am going to try to set it all down.

To my mind there can be no doubt that Sir Winston Churchill stands above the other great figures of our time. Whose achievements can rank with his? Oddly enough, proximity did not lessen his magnitude.

We of his personal staff were called upon to put forth the maximum effort of which our frames, nerves and minds were capable. I do not think this was only because it was wartime; I believe he has always been a fairly exacting employer. He has, to make use of one of his favourite adjectives, a prodigious capacity for work and, in those days at any rate, he expected those around him to devote themselves heart and soul to the cause to which he had dedicated himself. Perhaps he did this unconsciously—certainly to serve him satisfactorily one had to be willing to blot out all other interests and occupations.

I think I used to grumble sometimes that there was never any opportunity for dates or fixing one's clothes. But it did not go very deep. From first to last we were utterly devoted to him, not because he was Prime Minister but because he was himself. Mr. Churchill—as I shall now continue to call him, for so it was that I knew him—was a hero to his staff, and particularly to his female staff. He was a person whom it was quite safe to hero-worship, for if one had not done so one could hardly have borne the effort involved in giving him satisfactory service. Certainly to me he shone with a very, very bright light. Perhaps, after all, it was the unheroic in him that endeared him to us—his twinkling eye and occasional jests at the expense of ourselves or the Private Secretaries, his unselfconsciousness,

---

1. This was penned before the release of the first edition in 1958.

his extravagant love for the cat, for instance—the emotion he would feel on hearing of the exploits of Royal Naval ships, his beaming smile of thanks when he was aware that one had stayed up all night fair-copying a speech.

I do not think there were many who in those days would have wished to devote more than a few years of life to serving Winston Churchill, as in time a state of complete exhaustion would have been reached; but I know that anyone who has had the privilege of working on his staff must feel for ever a different person, must feel that he or she has passed close to a personality not to be met with again. What is the key to his character? Wherein lies the focal point of his greatness? I have always thought it is more than anything else his courage.

In this account of my adventures during those war years I shall try only to let you see events as I saw them. I shall not presume to attempt any summing up, nor any broad appreciation of Winston Churchill, nor do I feel that any comments on the prosecution of the war are called for from me. I shall stick to the sphere in which I worked. If in these pages there is found frequent repetition of the words "I" and "my" it cannot be helped: otherwise I cannot write anything. But these events are written down because they happened, and not because they happened to me.

Among the many young women who have taken dictation from him during his long lifetime, I do not think Winston Churchill would remember me particularly. Perhaps he might recall the evening when a Russian General dumped a bunch of flowers unceremoniously in my lap by way of a bouquet. But I cannot, could not forget him and, after reading through the letters and records that I scribbled off to my mother to remind myself in time to come, those days do not seem very far off.

Here, then, is what happened to me.

1

I was born in England, in the old-fashioned little town of Bury St. Edmunds, Suffolk, where long ago the nobles conferred before making King John sign the Magna Carta. But when I was seven years old my father, who was recovering from T.B. of the lungs consequent on the First World War, was told that for the sake of his health he must leave England for good. He was given a choice of two places to move to—South Africa or British Columbia; and after some thought he decided on the latter. Therefore in August of 1924 we sailed away for Canada.

We were brought up in the most wonderful country in the world, the western slopes of the Rocky Mountains, in the Okanagan Valley, famed for its apples. It was a happy, unsophisticated, uncomplicated sort of life. We lived on the shore of a beautiful lake, and each day in summer would throw ourselves several times into its cool water. When the winter freeze-up came and snow and ice appeared, out would come our skates and toboggans, and, when we got bigger, our skis. My mother did the cooking and made all our clothes. My sister and I had little jobs to do about the house after school, and my brother helped my father in the garden and with picking the fruit when the season came round. Once a year, during the summer holidays, we would drive to the city of Vancouver, some three hundred and sixty miles off, where we were entranced with the bright lights and the busy city life.

I didn't know what I wanted to do in the world—but I wanted to do something. While I was passionately attached to the lovely country in which we lived, perhaps there were times when I felt a bit different from our country-fellows and longed to see again the old world which I could still remember. I finished school rather early, and stayed quietly at home for a couple of years—earned a little money and bought myself a horse, a much-loved addition to the family circle. Then my father decided it was time I did some work, and so in 1936 he sent me to London for a secretarial course.

It was the greatest thrill in the world. I was completely the country mouse come to town, and I tramped miles and miles around the great city, learning the whereabouts of the famous places. After the secretarial course, which lasted the best part of a year, I was offered a job in the employment bureau connected with the College, for it seemed that I had done well and had proved an apt pupil in the arts of shorthand and typewriting and office procedure, in which I was now most thoroughly versed.

To be quite honest, I was a little disappointed that I was still to work within the ægis of the College, which was a world of women, instead of launching out into the world of business—but the employment bureau was situated in the City of London proper, and there were great new fields for exploration during my lunch hours, many of which were spent in gazing on the Pool of London from London Bridge and wondering what happened, when the Tower Bridge opened to let river traffic pass, to those who might have strayed across the river during the lunch-hour and would now be late in returning to their offices. I toured the City churches most energetically, and sometimes climbed the 365 steps of the Monument, to gaze out over the City. In addition to these new interests, I was assured that to work in the College's City office was an honour and a chance which would prove a good investment in days to come, when I should be seeking other work. How true this was to prove!

So two years passed happily and busily. I lived in a boarding-house in West Cromwell Road, and sometimes I had a boy friend to escort me out at night, sometimes not. In the summer of 1939, having saved up hard, I went back to British Columbia for a holiday, meaning to return after three months to find myself a new job in the world of men, where no doubt I should meet someone tall and brave, and life would be settled.

But then war broke out, and everyone's plans went haywire. I longed to return to London and help with the business of fighting the war, but now domestic complications set in and I was urgently needed at home to look after my mother. This position lasted until halfway through 1940, when I found myself free once more to leave home and return to England. But now, alas, it seemed it was too late; a letter to Ottawa requesting permission to book a passage to London produced a polite but firm reply that no women, unless in uniform, and therefore in the service of the Canadian Government, were allowed to leave Canada for the United Kingdom.

I felt considerably dashed, but after some months of reflection decided I could not leave it like that. I had been a member of the A.R.P. (Air Raid Precautions) organization in London during the year following Munich, and had spent much time in study and in assembling and distributing gas masks—respirators, as they were called. And now I wanted to use that training. I wanted to share the lot of the Londoners who had been my comrades. Let's be honest, I felt bored with safety and wanted to join in all the excitement.

After overcoming some opposition at home I withdrew my entire bank balance, took a one-way tourist-class ticket to Ottawa, and presented myself so persuasively to the Under-Secretary who had written the letter that he revised my case and authorized me to sail from St. John—saying more or less, "If you want to commit suicide, that's your own business." This was in early December.

We had a very stormy crossing, travelling alone—that is, without convoy—in a small Belgian cargo vessel. At one stage the tossing was so violent that a lifeboat jumped its moorings and hung over the side of the ship, where it banged to and fro, alarming the passengers considerably. It was cut loose and later seen by the enemy, for the German radio reported that S.S. *Leopoldville* had been sunk. Indeed, the ship before us was torpedoed, and also the one after us, but we passed through a nest of five U-boats unnoticed—perhaps the storm had upset their tummies too. Some days later we reached Gourock, in the Clyde River.

The harbour was an unforgettable sight. It was our first real touch of the war, and it made us aboard very thoughtful. The place was filled with derelict ships, victims of bombing attacks or of U-boat warfare. Everywhere masts or funnels protruded from the water. All around us were shattered-looking cargo vessels, some visibly damaged, others floating at peculiar angles, a few still in seemingly seaworthy condition. I stood on deck, gazing around at the harbour. It was reality, and it was depressing. I felt tired after the somewhat sleepless journey, suddenly apprehensive of what the future held, and at that moment, far from home and very much alone, wondering if I had done right. But then without warning the sun burst for a few minutes through the heavy clouds that were low above us, and the whole of Gourock harbour was illumined by a small but brilliant rainbow. It seemed a good sign, and it dispelled my gloom.

Disembarking at Glasgow, we passed through the Customs. I was highly delighted when a Customs official, finding I had but a few pounds to my name, offered to lend me some money! Actually on reaching London I had twenty-five shillings left.

My first call was of course upon my friends in the employment bureau where I had worked, with an urgent request for a job. It so happened that the night before there had been an exceedingly heavy fire blitz, buildings were still ablaze, the streets were running with water from the fire hoses, and my friends were sitting somewhat woefully in their offices in a state of semi-emergency. They were considerably astonished to see me, and wondered greatly that I should have made such efforts to return to the battered city of London. They promised to find me something interesting, directly connected with the war, and in the meantime I started work the same day for the Prisoners of War Department of the Red Cross, which eased the financial crisis.

Little did I guess what lay ahead.

And here I must pause to tell you about London as it was then. The worst of the Blitz was past; but almost every night raiders arrived. Air raids were not as alarming as my imagination had pictured them; perhaps that was because I was never involved in a hit. I lived with some friends in a large block of flats and three of us—Audrey and Peter from neighbouring flats, and I—formed a fire-extinguishing team under the local A.R.P. Warden. We possessed a fine stirrup-pump, and when the warning siren sounded we had to leap out of bed and prepare for action while other residents hurried downstairs to the shelter. I must admit we were never called on to put out a fire, but it made us feel important.

Sometimes we would be up all night. For those who have never experienced an air raid, I give the following extract from my diary of that time:

"Tonight we received the heaviest weight of bombs yet to be dropped upon us in one go. Jerry began to arrive about nine o'clock, and at first concentrated upon the eastern parts of the City. The others began going downstairs, but Audrey and I, who were not on duty that night, decided to go to bed. About midnight some loud cracking noises woke me, and I found the room was light as day; outside hung a brilliant cluster of marking lights, a 'chandelier'. The roar of the guns came very close, and every few minutes the whole building would tremble and sway as a bomb fell not far off. Audrey and I in great excitement rushed up to the sixth floor and gazed from the windows. Away to the east we could see seven distinct patches of angry red; the docks were afire. Nearer, other fires were starting. The bells of fire-engines hurrying by could be heard. The drone of aircraft sounded just above our heads. The guns roared continuously. We saw a great flash a little way ahead, and immediately a huge mushroom of smoke arose. This was a land-mine exploding. We felt the girders of the block rubbing against each other as the building rocked and, a bit scared, we ran downstairs. Someone came in with the cheering report that gas had been dropped, but it wasn't true. We hurried about trying to keep the old girls calm with cups of tea, and fooling around to make them laugh. About three o'clock I went to bed again. But I couldn't sleep: the sound of a car coming quickly down the road outside was too much like the soft whistling rush that a bomb makes as it falls, and the memory of that great mushroom of smoke was too distinct. That night Jerry only went home at six o'clock."

In the mornings Audrey and I would catch a bus together to get to work, and frequently there would be diversions of the route, as many of the streets would be out of use. I remember walking one morning to St. James's Palace, where the Red Cross was housed. Piccadilly was closed to motor traffic, and the roadway was piled high with glass and full of craters; from the Ritz Hotel in Piccadilly to the Mall there was a long line of flames and smoke—a terrible sight. St. James's Palace had been hit and was burning slightly; however, the damage there was not too serious and work carried on as usual.

It was quite an experience in those days to travel on the Underground after seven in the evening. You would find the whole station—the moving staircase, the approach to the platform, the platform itself—choked with people arriving to spend the night underground. There were double-decker bunks, and these all had their proper tenants. Spaces on the stone floor were reserved from night to night for regular shelterers, who would arrive with a blanket and pillow, or a coat and a hot-water bottle, or sometimes with nothing at all. You would see some people sitting up and chatting, some lying asleep, arms shielding their eyes, some prowling about in search of buns and tea which were sold by girls in white aprons and caps. All the time traffic proceeded in and out as usual, the passengers stepping carefully over the rows of recumbent forms while the trains shot noisily past. I believe the shelterers became quite hardened to sleeping in these conditions and almost grew to enjoy the communal life. I found travelling underground depressing and used the buses whenever possible.

It was into this rather muddled existence that the great news suddenly fell upon me. A telephone call from the employment bureau—the Prime Minister needs an additional shorthand-typist on his staff and would you like to apply? *Would* I? Luckily they did not send any other applicants, and I was taken on. I felt rather like one of the barrage balloons that floated over London.

2

On the 5th May, 1941, I started work at 10 Downing Street—No. 10, as it is always called by those who work there. The Street was closed to the general public, and being rather childish I was impressed to be bowed through by the policeman on duty, who had been forewarned of my arrival.

There stood the door so often seen in photographs. Plain, black, with a bell on one side, the figures 10 in the centre and a lionhead knocker. It was opened by a uniformed doorman, and I stepped into the entrance hall, where a policeman also stood on duty. A Messenger (or man-servant) appeared—tall, unobtrusive and perfectly mannered—and conducted me down a long red-carpeted passage which led to a lobby outside the Cabinet Room. In a small open space on one side of the passage a bust stood upon a pedestal—I never did find out whose head it was.

In the red-carpeted lobby I saw the door to the Cabinet Room, the nerve centre of the British Government these last two hundred years. Beside it stood a solid-looking grandfather-clock with a solemn tick. To the left was the Prime Minister's study, and to the right one turned off to the Private Secretaries' office and farther to the room used by the Personal Secretaries. In doing so one passed a row of hooks on the wall, each one with a notice above it denoting which Cabinet Minister was to hang his hat and coat thereon.

As a building No.10 appeared plain and old-fashioned—almost snobbish in its unpretentiousness. Over it there hung an air of quiet, dignity and respect, of age and tradition, of well-trained servants and an absolute routine of service. One did not, for instance, feel inclined to burst into song and try out the odd dance step. One felt at once hushed and a little awed, and honoured to be there.

I was shown the Cabinet Room, the Prime Ministerial party having not yet arrived from Chequers. From the lobby it was reached by a pair of doors, two together, the outer of which was covered with green baize to exclude noise—or perhaps it was to include noise. I saw a large oblong room with windows to the north and west looking over the garden of No.10 and beyond that to the Horse Guards Parade, for the ground falls away from Downing Street and the Cabinet Room is on the first floor. Around the walls were bookcases filled with leather-bound volumes, mostly Hansard, and a map of the world. There was a big rectangular table about which were placed some twenty-two leather-seated and backed chairs, each of which I was told had its regular occupant by office. The chair for the Prime Minister, the only one with arms, was in the centre of the long side of the table nearer to the door, and behind this was the fireplace, over which hung the only picture in the room, a portrait of Sir Robert Walpole, the first Prime Minister of Britain, who held that office from 1721 to 1742. On the mantel stood a large clock, an apparatus showing the date and a jar containing a small bunch of white heather, which I was told had recently been sent to Mr. Churchill for luck. Otherwise the room contained no ornaments.

Mr. Churchill's place at the table was marked by an interesting array of buzzers, pens, pencils, tags for joining papers, a paper punch for making holes for the tags, and some red labels stating "Action This Day". Standing on a table at the side was a covered typewriter, which I was told would be placed on the table opposite his seat when he wished to dictate.

To the right of the door as one came in were large double doors leading to the Private Secretaries' office, which in turn led to the Personal Secretaries' office beyond.

And here let me explain the secretarial position at No.10 at that time. There were six Private Secretaries, five men and one woman, who were Civil Servants, officially appointed. They occupied positions of considerable standing and did not necessarily change with a change of Prime Minister. Four of the men, probably in their late twenties or early thirties, took turns at being actively on duty, usually two at a time. This meant that they acted as a buffer between Mr. Churchill and the rest of the world, seeing to his requirements, receiving information for him, guarding the precious Boxes in which his work was kept. Besides this, of course, they had a great deal of correspondence to deal with on his behalf, reports to produce according to the particular interest of each one, and many papers to read through each day in order to keep abreast of all that came in and went out. The fifth male Private Secretary worked more behind-scenes and advised the Prime Minister on various matters, and Miss Watson, a great character who had been at No.10 for about twenty years, dealt with vast quantities of correspondence from the general public.

To be appointed Private Secretary to the Prime Minister was an honour which would surely lead to a distinguished career. Their work called for the highest degree of care and responsibility, and their first-rate education and high office combined to give them plenty of self-confidence. Coming from the backwoods of Canada I at first found these elevated gentlemen slightly alarming. However, I soon discovered that they in their turn were somewhat overawed by the Prime

Minister, and told myself that they were only passing on a discomfiture which perhaps they resented.

Mr. Churchill greatly disliked any change of staff. Specially he disliked a new typist—or shorthand-writer, which was the official term—in fact, at times it would put him off his work to see a strange face opposite him. He had, therefore, on his return to office in 1939, brought with him the two women who had been his secretaries at Chartwell, his home in Kent, when he was a private individual, and had declined to make use of the services of the considerable number of young women Civil Servants, who should by rights have been going in to him by rota for dictation on all official matters. These two former, now known as his Personal Private Secretaries (or Personal Secretaries), had been flogging themselves ever since to serve him night and day, whenever dictation was required—and this might be at any hour, for any length of time—dealing with his personal work such as family affairs, personal letters, constituency business, household accounts, gifts and photographs, which should have been their sole function, as and when they could. There may have been some slight resentment felt by the official staff at this arrangement, though in general the attitude was "Anything that makes his task the least bit lighter is gladly accepted".

The time had now arrived, however, when these two Personal Secretaries felt they could keep going no longer—and a third was to be added. This was myself. This would not, they told me, be a popular decision with Mr. Churchill, but they themselves being only mortal it was a necessary one.

It was explained to me that No.10 was not at present being used as the official residence of the Prime Minister and Mrs. Churchill. It is an old building, badly constructed from the first in that it is two houses knocked into one, and when the Treasury (next door) had been hit by a bomb, No.10 had been shaken so as to make it unsafe for the Prime Minister's use in case of further air raids. Another building, the Annexe, had therefore been prepared for him; it was about five minutes' walk from No.10 at Storey's Gate, facing St. James's Park and flanked by Great George Street, and here were also housed the offices of the War Cabinet and the Service Planning Staffs. For Mr. and Mrs. Churchill and the household staff there was a flat more or less at ground level, small but comfortably furnished, where they lived and slept. Within the flat was an office shared by the Personal Secretaries and Mrs. Churchill's Secretary. The location of the flat was not ideal, as it was situated between the main door to the building and the offices of the Prime Minister's official staff, and the traffic along the carpeted passage (which incidentally was flanked by Mr. Churchill's own paintings) and through the swing door at the other end was constant, almost embarrassingly so. But it was wartime, and in other respects the building was suitable.

For below it there stretched two whole floors of "safety" accommodation. Beneath a vast concrete block which had been set in at ground level there was first of all General Headquarters, known as the Cabinet War Room or C.W.R., where the Prime Minister, all Cabinet Ministers and the Chiefs of Staff had rooms as well as the Service Planning Staffs. Here some of the most brilliant British officers spent their days breathing conditioned air and working by daylight lamps, to emerge white-faced and blinking for a few hours in the evening. The C.W.R. was reached by a spiral staircase and was supposed to be safe from bombing attack. Below it, on a still lower level, had been constructed a whole floor of tiny bedrooms for the lesser lights, each with its allocated owner, and it was here that those on late duty would retire when bedtime came.

Mr. Churchill could hardly ever be persuaded to descend to the C.W.R. merely for "sheltering" purposes. He often held Cabinet meetings there in the evenings, after which he would return to the ground-level flat to finish off the evening in his study. I never knew him use his bedroom belowstairs—thick steel shutters guarded the window of his bedroom in the flat, and these he felt sufficient protection.

During the daytime he would spend as much time as possible at No.10, preferring the old, historic building. Therefore a duplicate set of offices for the Private and Personal Secretaries was needed. Somewhat against the advice of those around him, he would whenever possible have his appointments arranged at No.10—Cabinet meetings held during the day were always there, and sometimes, particularly as the war progressed, late meetings (which would start at 10.30) would also be held there. There was a small shelter which was supposed to be completely safe—I entered it only once, as I shall later recount.

No.10 was for the most part closed, except for the ground floor, though Mrs. Hill, who was the senior Personal Secretary, and Miss Hamblin, who was Mrs. Churchill's Secretary, still used their bedrooms on the second floor. Below the Cabinet Room level some small rooms had been fitted out as an alternate flat for the Prime Minister's use—for entertaining only, not for sleeping purposes—and one of our urgent duties each morning was to find out where meals and appointments for the day were to be held. Much of our time was spent in trotting between the two offices, and confusion was frequently caused when visitors failed to make sure of the rendezvous. The kitchen staff would wail in despair when dinner turned out to be "at the other side", and a hurried exit with dishes and baskets of food would take place.

All this was explained to me by Mrs. Hill and her assistant, who went on to tell me about working conditions. The hours worked by the Prime Minister were, they said, rather unusual, though not really different from the hours he had kept when they worked privately for him at Chartwell. He was, they said, an unusual man. Mr. Churchill would usually waken about 8 o'clock, and would have breakfast in bed on a tray. During this meal he would read through all the morning papers—perhaps he didn't read every word, but he always had a good idea of what each contained, and noticed if one was missing. Thereafter, having lighted up his first cigar, he would recline in bed propped up with pillows, dressed in his favourite dressing-gown, which was green and gold with red dragons on it, and work on his Box, the key of which, on a long silver chain, never left him. This was a rectangular black box which locked automatically on closing—there were a good number of such about the office—and "Gimme my Box" was a phrase we all knew well. Inside were various folders, always in their prescribed order. The first contained particularly urgent papers, such as telegrams from President Roosevelt or Marshal Stalin, or from the Generals in the field; the second, Foreign Office telegrams; then Service telegrams, Cabinet papers, etc. It was always prepared by the Private Secretaries and placed on a stool next to his bed, key on the bed-table, so that as soon as he awoke in the morning he could open it if he wished.

Mr. Churchill found it more restful to work in bed, and because of the great calls upon his strength he was urged by his medical advisers to do so as often as possible. He would remain there until half an hour before his first appointment, sometimes receiving visitors but often working the entire morning at his Box. Half an hour was always allowed for bathing and dressing, and the day would vary according to the business written on the Card, a large white square with a space for each day of the month, on which all appointments were recorded. Luncheon was invariably at 1.30, and every day at some time before dinner, which was at 8.30, he would have a sleep of at least an hour, from which he would awake refreshed and ready—which perhaps his staff were not—for another normal day's work before bedtime. This was very seldom before 2 o'clock and might be anything up to 4.30. "It's amazing," they told me, "how quickly you get used to going to bed at 2.30."

It was also explained that working for the Prime Minister was not easy, particularly at first. As I have said, he did not like new staff and would be looking for a reason to lodge an objection. In those days he was in the habit of dictating straight on to the typewriter in order to save time, the war being most anxious and pressing. One used a noiseless typewriter, and as he finished dictating one was to hand over the Minute, letter or directive ready for signing, correct, unsmudged, complete. He would then sign or initial it, buzz for the Private Secretary, and it would be dispatched, frequently topped with the bright red sign stating "Action This Day" already mentioned.

But, they told me, it's not easy to hear what he says. He has a very slight impediment in his speech connected with the letter S, and that, combined with the ticking of the typewriter, makes for difficulty. Until you get used to his voice it's almost impossible to catch everything. There's always that cigar, and usually he paces up and down the room as he dictates, so that sometimes he's behind your chair and sometimes far across the room. You must be prepared to go fast in short bursts, to finish one sentence before he starts another—and for Heaven's sake don't make any typing errors. When you don't hear you may ask him what he said, if you're brave and prepared for a squash; or you may put what you thought he said, if you don't mind having your head snicked off; or you may leave a space and hope that from the sense you'll later realize what it was you missed, in which case you can creep back quietly on the typewriter and put it in—and hope he doesn't roar at you for fidgeting. There's always a rubber eraser attached to every typewriter, but don't be so rash as to fidget by using it. You must take two carbon copies of everything you type, but don't rustle the paper while you are preparing it. In any case you're bound to have it a bit rough at first, and if you'd rather leave now you can still do so.

I thought I'd have a try.

For the next few weeks, therefore, I worked in the office under the two Personal Secretaries. I learned how Mr. Churchill liked his Minutes typed, always in double spacing with a space left at the bottom for his initials and the date in figures under that. I learned how to do Speech Form, the way he liked his speeches and broadcasts typed out—a special method he had evolved through the years with various recognized abbreviations and the lines arranged in phrases so that the finished product looked rather like hymn sheets. Fortunately I found I could do this from the start—either one could or one couldn't. I was told that if there was a choice of "z" or "s" in spelling, he liked the old-fashioned "z". I was told that if the Prime Minister said "Gimme Pug" I must fetch General Ismay, his constant adviser on military affairs and Secretary to the Chiefs of Staff Committee, whose pleasant face did have a slightly puggish look; that if he said "Gimme Prof" I must go and ask for Lord Cherwell, his scientific adviser; and that if he merely stretched out his hand and said "Gimme" I must be so well in sympathy with the train of his thought as to be able to place in his hand whatever he needed from a selection of black pen, red pen, tag (for joining sheets of paper), paper punch for making holes therein—which object he called a Klop—blotting paper, "Action This Day" label or brush and water for wetting same preparatory to sticking—and so on.

(The above is written rather light-heartedly. In general, any fetching of visitors or putting through of telephone calls was done by the Private Secretary on duty.)

There was, of course, other work to be done besides taking dictation. There was the secretarial side—writing short letters on the Prime Minister's behalf in respect of personal matters, and drafting personal letters for his signature, doing the household accounts, keeping the files, helping Miss Hamblin with Mrs. Churchill's correspondence, and so on. And there were other, to me, more interesting tasks which fell to my lot, being the junior—taking the Prime Minister's glasses to be repaired, or going to the bank for the weekly household wages, or getting a book from the library for his reference, or fetching something for Mrs. Churchill from Bond Street. On such occasions one was treated with great respect by those whom one visited, which I enjoyed, being, as I have said, still childish.

This was the background to which I became accustomed during those first weeks. Of course one could not help knowing when He was "in" and when He was "out"—when bells and buzzers had an urgent note, when the air tingled and Messengers hurried on tiptoe, when Private Secretaries looked harassed and spoke in hushed tones, when a whiff of cigar smoke reached one and perhaps an occasional rumble of anger was heard through closed doors, then one knew the Prime Minister was at home. Once or twice I caught a glimpse of him; I began to long to take the plunge and get started.

3

When three weeks later the time came for me to be tried out for dictation, I knew the others were a bit anxious on my behalf. I was full of confidence, insisting I was ready to begin, and could not altogether appreciate why they should feel thus. I soon found out.

One night I was left on duty. Usually on an evening when there was no meeting the Prime Minister would start working on his Box at about 10.30, frequently with one or two of his close friends keeping him company or giving him the information he required from their particular sphere. When he reached some business upon which he wished to dictate he would buzz for the Private Secretary and request a Shorthand-writer, or a Young Woman, who would then sit behind the noiseless typewriter (there was one kept in every room in which he ever worked) typing as required, until bedtime. He seldom asked for any of us by name.

On this occasion I waited, was at last summoned, and entered his study feeling rather like someone who is about to be decapitated. And there he was, at last, the man in whose hands our future rested. He was pacing the room, cigar in mouth. He was not as big as I had thought he would be, but fairly plump, compact, controlled, forceful as he strode up and down. I noticed his well-shaped head and high forehead, his pinkish skin which had a healthful look, the smooth dome of his head. He was wearing his siren suit, an Air-Force blue garment shaped like a boiler suit with a zip up the front, originally designed for the raids, a garment which had become very popular with him. (It was called in the office, I am sorry to say, his rompers.)

He gave me a sharp look but made no remark. I sat at the typewriter and presently he began dictating, still pacing the room. All machines were always left in readiness at double spacing, but as I hurried on to the second line, too late I found this one had been switched over to single spacing. It was too late to change now, so I continued in single spacing. Here, on my first try, I'd muffed it.

It was not long before, passing behind the typewriter, he noticed the single spacing. At once he went off like a rocket. I was a fool, a mug, an idiot: I was to leave his presence and one of the others was to appear.

Naturally this was rather upsetting. After a few days I tried again. Let us not go through this period in detail. For some weeks I seemed unable to do anything right. Perhaps it was that having only recently come from Canada I was not well up with current affairs; perhaps I should not have gone so soon to him for dictation but should have spent some months working in the office first—had the other two been less tired and less anxious for a relief no doubt I should have had to do so. Each time I was on duty I would sit in great anxiety, frantically remembering all the things they had told me to help me. When I had finished typing a Minute I would pass it over for signature expecting the worst. My apprehensions were seldom ill-founded. More often than not it would come skimming back to me with a few red alterations on it, for retyping, sometimes to the accompaniment of remarks disparaging to my education and sense of hearing.

Let me say at once that neither I nor anyone else considered this treatment unfair. The Prime Minister carried a terrific load; he was the spearhead of our stand against Nazism. The war was hard and heavy—we had just lost Crete—and he had a right to expect perfect service from those given the honour of being attached to him (though in all truth no one who served him was exempt from being jumped on now and then). I used to wonder how long his patience would last, if he would not one day say, "Go, and never let me see you again." It was just a trying period for *anyone* to go through, and I was lucky enough to be that anyone.

The others stood by and comforted when they could. Mrs. Hill told me how when she had first worked for him at Chartwell he had told her "Gimme Klop", whereat much to his astonishment she had brought in fifteen volumes of an encyclopdia by a gentleman named Kloppe which she had noticed in his library, when he merely wanted the paper punch. General Ismay, who was always kind and friendly towards us, told me a wonderful story. One night, he said, the P.M. had been dictating about future operations, and operational code-names, which were always typed in block capitals, were several times mentioned. The Prime Minister, in speaking of the Greek islands, made a remark about Lemnos, but when the sheets were handed over he was surprised to read (according to General Ismay) that "LEMONS could be picked up cheap today".

And then good fortune came to my aid; the second of the Personal Secretaries caught the measles, and the Prime Minister had no alternative but to put up with my services every day, since anyone else would have been even less familiar. I felt encouraged, and even more determined. It was perhaps a little disappointing when one day Mr. Churchill decided to go to Chartwell for a night or so, and, oh delight, I was to go, too: but coming from the Cabinet Room, beaming with pleasure to be off to his loved house, he saw me ready with my hat on and his face fell yards. "Oh, are *you* coming?" he said in dismay.

I have often laughed since to think how seriously I took these things at the time. He did not mean to be unkind. He was just heart and soul engaged in winning the war.

The second Personal Secretary was away some time and Mrs. Hill took me each weekend to Chequers, the country home of the Prime Minister of Great Britain, near Aylesbury, Buckinghamshire, where the Churchills went regularly each Friday afternoon until Monday morning. This weekly expedition provided a change which the Prime Minister enjoyed, and which gave him more peace than he would have had in town. It was also an opportunity for him to entertain and consult with, in more informal surroundings, those on whom he relied for information, advice and help in the prosecution of the war, his own chosen Ministers and Service Chiefs as well as visitors from overseas.

Here the atmosphere in the office was more informal, and one gained a little confidence from seeing Mr. Churchill relaxed and at ease. Here, too, many of his speeches and broadcasts were first drafted, and dictation of this kind was never so difficult.

I found that the Prime Minister's dictation seemed to fall into three types. First, speeches and broadcasts. When he was first drafting these he would frequently make alterations: the thing had to be retyped several times anyway, plenty of crossings-out would appear and sentences written above the line; therefore one did not need to be as particular as usual, though one always kept a rough tally of how many words had been dictated, to have an answer ready for the sudden demand "How much so far?" The second kind, a long directive or perhaps a telegram to the President, had to be typed with care since he would wish to sign or initial it on completion, but was not too difficult as one knew what was the subject on hand and could follow the trend of his thought. The third type, which was where I used to run into difficulties, was dictation on the matters in his Box. One would have not the slightest idea what he was reading, and suddenly out of the blue a Minute would be shot out at one on any subject under the sun. Sometimes that cigar would seem to get in the way of some of the words: one might perhaps feel what one handed over was correct, but back it would come with the information, impatiently given, that the time was "ripe" rather than "right", or that he had dictated "fretful" and why had I put "dreadful"?

I made plenty of inexcusable mistakes, also, chiefly from anxiety. I remember once putting "since time immemorable" instead of "immemorial", which was rather poorly received, and never having heard of General Auchinleck I made a hash of spelling his name the first time, which gave considerable pain. When on another occasion the Prime Minister said something about "the importance of chrome in this connection", my mind went blank and I put Crome as if it had been a man ... "What, *never heard of chrome!*" I wrote "perverted" instead of "perfervid", and many other such slips.

I had been working regularly for Mr. Churchill for about six weeks, toiling anxiously onward, looking a little long-faced and depressed, when suddenly my corner was turned. One weekend he was to prepare an enormous address to the House of Commons on the subject of Production—in the end it was 10,000 words. We were at Chequers, and on the Saturday evening after a cinema show he came into the office and sent me for a walk in the garden, saying I'd need some air. About one o'clock he called me into the Hawtrey Room, a lovely place which he often used for work, and dictated, this time for shorthand, without stopping until 4.30.

On these occasions he would walk up and down the room, his forehead crinkled in thought, the cords of his dressing-gown trailing behind him (he often wore his favourite red, green and gold dressing-gown when dictating). Sometimes he would fling himself for a moment into a chair: sometimes he would pause to light his cigar, which with so much concentration was neglected and frequently went out. For minutes he might walk up and down trying out sentences to himself. Sometimes his voice would become thick with emotion, and occasionally a tear would run down his cheek. As inspiration came to him he would gesture with his hands, just as one knew he would be doing when he delivered his speech, and the sentences would roll out with so much feeling that one died with the soldiers, toiled with the workers, hated the enemy, strained for Victory.

During this particular session he stopped once to ask if I were tired, and when I told him I was not, he said, "We must go on and on like the gun-horses, till we drop." It was an easy matter to produce a correct transcript of dictation into shorthand, since without the patter of the typewriter and in the absence of haste one seemed able to hear what he said with the greatest ease.

This occasion produced twenty-seven pages of typescript—double spacing, of course—a substantial part of the final speech. Much mirth was caused around the office when it was noticed that I had inadvertently put "he had even heard it said that the Air Minister was in a state of chaos from top to bottom" (instead of Ministry), but they told me this was the only mistake.

After that weekend I think Mr. Churchill felt confidence in me, and I certainly seemed to have found confidence in myself, for though he was to roar at me again on many occasions it never went very deep, and I knew now that I was accepted as one of his staff.

Not long after this episode the second of the Personal Secretaries left, and I found to my surprise I was now the Assistant Personal Secretary to the Prime Minister. It did seem rather an amazing consequence of that uncomfortable Atlantic crossing less than a year before. During the next year or so various young women came and went as the third on our staff. One was found in due course to have slight T.B., presumably as a result of constant sleeping underground: another had a nervous breakdown—she was a nervous type anyway; yet another was put off by an initial error in her work. It needed a fair determination to keep going, and many times did I bless my healthy Canadian upbringing.

4

The Atlantic Meeting, which took place shortly after the incidents I have outlined and of which much has been written elsewhere, was a big event in our lives, the first coming together of the two great Heads of States, Prime Minister Churchill and President Roosevelt. Our Principal Private Secretary, Mr. Martin, and the Naval Aide who acted as a Personal Assistant to the Prime Minister on the social side, Commander Thompson, were chosen from the office to accompany Mr. Churchill, and for dictation purposes a young man from another Government department, Peter Kinna, was roped in. No females—good Heavens, no!

We of the personal staff did not discuss such events even with each other until they were accomplished fact. It became second nature to keep the subject-matter of our dictation to ourselves even within the office, in cases where great secrecy was necessary. We felt it, of course, the highest honour to be entrusted with such secrets: I think it weighed upon us all. I remember wondering if the awful knowledge I had could be read in my face, and reminding myself not to glance at a map in passing in case I should somehow betray the scene of a coming operation.

I think we all knew that our personal histories were checked before we were allowed into the little circle, and that periodically we were followed by someone from Scotland Yard and our companions outside the office noted. In the case of the Personal Secretaries there was hardly any time to think of anything but work, and opportunities for social intercourse were very limited; but in any case there was really no danger of anything being given away by us: the responsibility lay too heavily upon us for any carelessness to have been possible, and devotion to our work went far too deep for there to be any desire to show off. Indeed, I do not think there was ever any cause for complaint about any member of the office staff regarding ill-advised talk.

At this time I was mainly doing night duties for the Prime Minister. Mrs. Hill arranged it, for the time being, that the other Young Woman and I should go alternate weekends with her to Chequers. On weekdays she would be on duty during the mornings, and for three days I would work the unusual hours of 2.30 in the afternoon until the Prime Minister went to bed; the other girl, who had other work to do in the office, did the fourth night spent in London. At Chequers Mrs. Hill would be with him in the mornings and whoever of us was with her would do the night duty, having worked in the office during the day. These arrangements were, of course, only approximate—frequently two of us would be required at the same time, and whenever a speech was in the offing it was a case of "all hands to the pumps".

This was a routine to which one quite soon adjusted oneself, just as they had told me. I still had my home in the flat of my friends in Kensington, and when in London and not sleeping in the shelter after late duty, I would go home to sleep, and sometimes pop home for an hour or two during the day. But I saw little of anyone outside the office except on my alternate free weekend—and that was, of course, a time for energetic washing and ironing of clothes. I grew used to spending three nights in a row on duty until 2 or 2.30, and sometimes later—and a night when we closed up promptly at 2 o'clock seemed quite adequate for rest. One would then retire to the second bathroom in the flat to put on one's night attire, taken from the suitcase from which one lived, and hurry down the two flights of twirly stairs, past the C.W.R., to the bedroom level below. By this time one was safe from meeting anyone, but when, having slept heavily for six hours, to the roar of the air-conditioning, in a narrow cot covered with Army blankets, one would be aroused by the alarm clock at 8.30 and emerge from one's room, there were all sorts of people about whom one wished to avoid. We had all fitted ourselves out with housecoats of the variety that displayed no signs of night attire, but somehow as one hurried up the twirly, draughty stairs in the morning, feeling heavy-eyed because the air-conditioning did not make for perfect sleeping conditions, one always met the most glamorous officers coming into the C.W.R., looking spruce and a bit haughty.

But we remembered, too, that it was wartime. I think our sense of proportion was better in those days—we *knew* it did not matter. Mr. Churchill would not have minded.

I became fond of my night duties. When we were at No.10 in the evenings I would sit at my desk there, finishing off little letters to constituents (always part of the personal staff's work), or thanking people for simple little presents they sent Mr. Churchill, or sticking his photographs in the big album—or sometimes writing to my mother, who could not be altogether neglected. There would be a Cabinet meeting, or an appointment with someone to whom the Prime Minister wished to talk—someone like General Smuts, Mr. Mackenzie King, Mr. Harry Hopkins, General Sikorski, the Pole, or one of our own Generals—and the hours would tick slowly past. There would be a hush over the old building, broken only by perhaps the cough of the Private Secretary on duty next door, the sound of the buzzer or telephone. Then suddenly a stir—the door from the Private Secretaries' room would open and one would be sent in for dictation.

Entering the Cabinet Room in these circumstances never failed to impress one as being a serious business. One would take one's folder of stationery, one's book and pencils, and go through the double doors from the Private Secretaries' room (never through the front door next to the clock, as this was for Ministers only), lift the typewriter from the table at the side, leaving the cover behind, and deposit it opposite Mr. Churchill's place, put the folder of stationery beside it and sit down as unobtrusively as possible. Sometimes one would be given a "Good evening", sometimes ignored. Sometimes there would be others in the room—one was never, of course, invited to enter while the Cabinet was still in session, though once or twice I was sent in just as they broke up and took down a long telegram with most of them watching and making comments or changes when invited.

At times one would sit opposite Mr. Churchill in the Cabinet Room for hours at a stretch, typing Minutes, directives or telegrams as required, and frequently merely sitting for long periods. At first I found it tiring merely waiting—trying to remain in readiness and mentally on tiptoe—but naturally as one became more used to the work it was possible to relax between spurts of dictation and think of other things. When it was a short note or Minute, Mr. Churchill would usually sit and rattle it off, holding out his hand for it almost before he had finished dictating, after which it would be "klopped" for attaching by a tag to the paper which had inspired it, and initialled. He had two regular pens—a beautiful gold one filled with blue-black ink with which he signed letters, and a "stylo" type one filled with red ink with which he initialled Minutes, directives and other documents, or ticked things he had merely read through. When it was something longer than a Minute, he would usually rise and walk up and down, working his cigar in his mouth and trying out a few sentences to himself. Then off he would go, the words would roll out, the gestures would start, and sometimes an emotional note would creep in. When he had finished that particular piece of business his mind would switch over completely to the next matter to be considered; he would sit down and return to his Box.

During these sessions in the Cabinet Room I found it pleasant to listen for the quarterly chimes of Big Ben, which in the quiet of the evening would be re-echoed back from the Admiralty building across the Horse Guards Parade, so that the sounds got mixed up. The Horse Guards clock also chimed quarterly, almost with Big Ben, but its cracked and tinkling note was distinctive.

Sometimes by the time bed was announced I would be feeling nervously worn out, especially if I'd made a few mistakes and come under the hammer that evening. But so often, Mr. Churchill would give a beaming "Good night", sometimes accompanied by a small remark intended to convey "Sorry I was cross", so that, far from resenting his previous displeasure, one would feel honoured to have been a sort of safety-valve for his feelings! Then one would walk back to the Annexe in the blackout—through the Foreign Office yard, where one sometimes fell over the sandbags which were piled about as blast protection, down the Clive Steps and along Storey's Gate—some five minutes—and so to the shelter.

The Prime Minister always seemed at his most approachable and considerate and easiest to work for when there was a crisis on, and one would have a feeling of sharing a tremendous experience with him. In calmer times, when there was less to worry about, he would sometimes be irritable and easily upset.

If the weather was bad or there was air-raiding, Mr. Churchill would not go to No.10 in the evening but would remain at the Annexe. Any meeting due to take place would be held in the C.W.R., and the rest of the evening would, as I have said, be spent in the study in the flat. This was not so thrilling as No.10, but it was cosier. Mr. Churchill seldom liked to be alone, but would have one or two of his close friends or advisers in attendance. Mr. Bracken of the newspaper world, later to be Minister of Information—tall, red-haired, bespectacled Mr. Bracken of the quick tongue—was a friend of many years; he would always be on tap until late at night in case called for by the Prime Minister. Mr. Eden (then Foreign Secretary) was, of course, our most constant visitor. On such informal occasions he would often be wearing a dark green velvet smoking jacket and black velvet slippers with his initials embroidered on the toes. (Mr. Churchill had a similar pair of which he was very fond, which were often a subject of comment by those who saw them for the first time and thought in error that the "W.S.C." was "P.M." upside-down.) Mr. Eden was always charming and considerate to us of the staff, far more approachable than Mr. Churchill; however, his dictation (which we sometimes received) seemed politely dull after what we were used to. I suppose he suffered from living in the shade of a mighty oak.

Mr. Attlee would sometimes be with Mr. Churchill in the evenings: he was Deputy Prime Minister of the Coalition Government, but by comparison (which is not really fair) he seemed rather colourless. Mr. Ernest Bevin was to me a great man in his own way. He reminded me of a steam shovel—no finesse but plenty of action.

Working at night at the Annexe was at least less lonely than being at No.10, for while one was waiting in the office there was always the household staff to entertain one—up to a certain time of night at any rate. We had a faithful household staff consisting of valet, cook, parlour-maid and house-maid. Labour was naturally a very difficult problem in those days, especially as much official entertaining had to be done, and these people were hard-worked. However, though well aware of their responsibilities, they were a cheerful crew and often made us laugh. Nellie, the parlour-maid, while essentially capable, was a nervous type. One evening she came running in from St. James's Park in great agitation, saying she had seen a man on top of the Admiralty building: obviously it must be a parachutist—"the Germans are coming!" We called for the guards and alerted the C.I.D., but it turned out that Nellie had seen Nelson on top of his column, nicely placed from where she stood. We teased her a good deal about this.

Another evening there was something of a domestic crisis. The Kents were coming to dinner in the flat, together with a few other guests, and Nellie's bones told her that something was sure to go wrong. It did. As she was passing the stewed raspberries, the Duke of Kent gestured with his hand in exactly the right direction and all the raspberries went down the back of the lady sitting next to him. I fear the dinner-party was somewhat spoilt—and for poor Nellie the whole sky was black for a week or so.

Mr. Churchill's valet-butler at that time was one Frank Sawyers, who was well known to most of the people with whom we came into contact. Though still quite young he was hairless, short and round, pale of face and somewhat toothless. He never managed to be quite on time, though with a rush and flurry at the last minute he avoided any major calamity. When out of The Presence he would often recapitulate incidents which had occurred while he was serving, which according to him arose chiefly from errors on the part of those he served. His gestures, combined with his lisp, made him very funny indeed. "Oh *Miss*," he would say, "and you know what he did next ...!" We laughed: but we were fond of him all the same. He was deeply attached to Mr. Churchill and a most faithful servant, remaining at his side wherever he went with almost never a day off. He had no interest in publicity for himself, but I am sure he could make a far better story than I.

He was the custodian of the famous cigars. Contrary to popular belief, which put the number at anything between thirty and fifty, Mr. Churchill did not smoke more than eight or ten cigars a day, but these lasted him all day. Indeed, he never seemed happy for a moment without a cigar between his lips unless it was mealtime. The cigars frequently went out, and vast quantities of large-size matches were used and a certain amount of time consumed in relighting them. They would burn along nicely at first, but then as their smoker's thoughts became fully engaged, their fire would die and they would be used merely as a sort of dummy—until their deficiency was noted and relighting performed. It was no good trying to palm off Mr. Churchill with anything but the best cigars, and Sawyers was always scurrying about to keep a sufficiency in store, all smokers' requirements being then in short supply. If some dealers were in the habit of keeping back their best Havana cigars for the P.M., who can blame them? He deserved it. Newcomers to his service might be surprised and a little alarmed when, a cigar proving not up to standard, the corpse would be hurled into the fire: old hands knew better than to sit between the Prime Minister and the fireplace, and so avoided the necessity of ducking.

One of the permanent mental pictures I have of Mr. Churchill is of the relighting of his cigar. A pause in whatever he was doing: the flame from a very large match jumping up and down, while clouds of blue smoke issued from his mouth; then a hasty shake of the match to extinguish it, and on with the job.

We of the personal staff were thrown together a great deal with Sawyers, Nellie and Mrs. Landemare the cook, a round body who could tell one in detail the intricacies of marriage and divorce among the aristocracy. We were all busy, all doing our best, all bothered when we slipped up. The feeling of comradeship with the household staff helped me to feel at home in the little circle. Mrs. Landemare gave me breakfast in the office each morning after late duty. Sawyers sometimes brought me a small glass of champagne when there was a dinner-party, or Nellie would produce an apple.

The front doors of the Annexe building opened almost directly upon St. James's Park, and on a summer evening, when one's own meal was over and Sawyers could assure one that, as so often happened, The Party had sat down late to dinner and would be engaged with dining and conversing for at least the next three-quarters of an hour, it would be the greatest happiness to stroll out into the Park and walk around the shores of the little lake. The pelicans would be standing hopefully in their usual spot at the eastern end. Countless tiny birds, making ready for bed, would be flying in groups about the island in the lake, squawking busily. And crossing the bridge which spans the lake, one would be hardly able to resist the appealing looks of the ducks of all varieties which floated below, imploring one to spare a crust of bread. To me it seemed the war did not touch St. James's Park, and one always returned refreshed.

Naturally one saw a great deal of Mrs. Churchill and the children. I often used to give a hand to her Secretary, Miss Hamblin—Ham, as we all called her. In fact, when once she went off for a week's leave I took her place as best I could. Mrs. Churchill was a beautiful and charming woman—beautiful of face and figure and beautifully dressed. Her vivacity and spirit made her a gay companion for the Prime Minister, and she contrived to bring a little of the normal into his busy life. They might indeed be quoted as an example of a happy marriage. She had a most alert mind and kept up to date with everything that went on, and sometimes Mr. Churchill would turn to her for advice of a practical nature. She was completely disinterested in publicity for herself, keeping in the background whenever possible, and immensely proud of her husband. A talented hostess who could put anyone at ease, she was also fluent in French. But I always felt Mrs. Churchill's main contribution to the greatness of her husband had been in standing up to him, in not being overwhelmed. Others might have spoilt him with adoration; she would not let him be selfish.

We saw a good deal of the daughters, too. Sarah, then about twenty-five, was an officer in the Women's Auxiliary Air Force (a W.A.A.F., one might say), and came when she could to see her parents. Mary, the youngest, was a Subaltern in the Auxiliary Territorial Service (the Women's Army), and had been posted to an Anti-Aircraft Battery in Hyde Park. When she had leave she would stay at the flat, and we took a great interest in her dresses and her "dates". She was a pretty girl with a gay and friendly smile. We saw less of Mrs. Duncan Sandys, the eldest daughter, and Randolph, who was on active service. All the "children" were devoted to their mother and to "Papa", as they called him.

As time went on I felt more and more deeply the honour and privilege of being taken into that household and accepted as one of them.

5

Work continued unceasingly, days passed, weeks, then months, and each day seemed to bring some fresh stimulation. I will not say "excitement", because that implies pleasure—and at that time of the war all the news seemed to be bad and never good. For me, getting used to the routine of the work and to appearing daily before Mr. Churchill, there were bad moments and good—bad when I felt I had irritated him by imperfect service, good when I was promoted to some new task and could feel I was gaining ground rather than losing.

I began to be aware of terrific deficiencies in my education. I had attended the local schools in Canada, so different from the English public schools for girls. I had not been to University. I could do shorthand and typing—and, yes, write letters; but by comparison with the great brain stored with knowledge under which we worked, I knew nothing, absolutely nothing at all. I began frantically to read books, at mealtimes in the little restaurants where we would go for lunch, or in the office canteen where we had supper in the evenings; sitting in St. James's Park during the morning after late duty; even when riding on buses to and from work. I read a number of *his* books, and felt thrilled to see the emergence and unrolling and building-up of his tremendous character revealed in his own writings.

For some weeks after her colleague left, Mrs. Hill did not have a day off but remained on duty every morning and hardly left the premises in case she was called for. Morning duties were the trickiest from our point of view. For some reason it was always more difficult to hear Mr. Churchill when he was sitting in bed—the double doors and heavily shuttered windows seemed to deaden his voice, or perhaps it was that at that time of the morning he did not feel so much inclined to articulate clearly. The time came when it was judged safe for her to take a day off during the week and for me to be on duty alone ... and one morning I duly presented myself at the Prime Minister's bedside at 8.30.

The routine was that one would not wait to be summoned, but would quietly enter the room when one judged he had finished breakfast and reading the newspapers, sit at the typewriter and, having arranged everything in readiness for dictation, make oneself as much a part of the furniture as possible. There would be small jobs to attend to—filling the pens, opening the Box, fetching Sawyers, etc. Sometimes Mr. Churchill would like to light his first cigar of the day with a candle, and then woe betide the one who forgot and blew the candle out instead of carrying it from the room, as the waxy smell was not popular. Frequently he was not in the best of moods at this time of day—perhaps from too little sleep—and added to this there was the hammering. Oh, that hammering!

The Annexe was still being converted to suit its occupants above and below ground, and during the day was full of workmen. While every effort was made to arrange for them to work in a part of the building far from the P.M.'s flat while he was there, there was always some clot who forgot the instructions and hammered in the wrong place. There would be a loud bang from somewhere, and one would stiffen as one saw Mr. Churchill look up. Peace. Then another bang or so, and knowing it was time for action one would leave the room hastily to have the hammerer stopped before the storm broke. The building was rather like a honeycomb, and sometimes it took our Royal Marine Messengers considerable time to find the seat of the trouble. This was never a good start to the day....

On this occasion to my great relief nothing untoward happened. The room seemed heavy with cigar smoke as I entered, and the Prime Minister, who was sitting propped up with pillows and wearing his favourite dressing-gown, looked gravely at me over his glasses—he wore them for reading only—but made no comment. For some months I found these morning sessions with the Box a considerable strain, particularly if, as often happened, his first appointment was luncheon and one was closeted with him from 8.30 until 1 o'clock. Later, when I had learned to relax a little, I found there was a certain comradely feeling, as Mr. Churchill was less impersonal than in the office, occasionally making a remark apart from his instructions—though, of course, he did not in any circumstances wish to hear a reply!

Certain expressions and customs had become part of everyday work. Very often Mr. Churchill would use the expression "pray". "Pray let me have a report"—"pray see there is no delay." Sometimes our forces, or those of the enemy, would meet with "a heavy prop", which was a stopping-blow. "The soft underbelly" was often mentioned, and "the Herrenvolk", the Nazis with their belief in their master-race. Certain words were unpopular; for instance, it must always be aircraft rather than aeroplane, airfield and not aerodrome. Certain words had always to receive a capital letter—Air, when used in the sense of Air cover or Air engagements, and usually the seasons and the points of the compass were spelt with a capital. And woe betide the one who put in a report containing a spelling error, which was never missed.

It was thoroughly understood throughout our circle that reports when called for should wherever possible be submitted on one side of a single sheet of paper, always in double spacing, to save time in perusal. As the Prime Minister read through the telegrams each day (Service and other telegrams which he would receive in the normal course of circulation), he would often pick out some slight decision or circumstance which he felt was wrong, and would instantly address a Minute inquiring into it. In this way he kept his finger on all aspects, both great and small, of the prosecution of the war. He was always roused to anger by any suspicion of slackness, lethargy or red-tape delay, and would dispatch a stinging Minute, which he would not forget to follow up if he did not at once receive a report in reply. His memory of what he had read and written was excellent, and he acted as a constant spur to those under him. Sometimes we could not help smiling when the recipient of one of these Minutes would turn up rather anxiously in the office bearing his reply (though in the normal course this would arrive in a locked box)—but it was, of course, the only way in which the Prime Minister could satisfy himself that his orders and wishes were being promptly and efficiently carried out, and after all it was he who bore the final responsibility for what happened.

Every few weeks he would deliver a Review of the War to the House of Commons, sometimes enormously long, sometimes less so. These speeches would take a great deal of preparation, and for a week beforehand we would all be aware that great things were astir—an egg was to be laid. As opportunity offered, a start would be made, perhaps part of the weekend would be devoted to breaking the back of the statement. Sometimes dictation would take place in the garden, and occasionally one would be required to follow Mr. Churchill around as he paced the lawn, scribbling hastily and awkwardly as one hurried after him. Usually the evening before the statement was due would be kept free for checking the final draft; two of the personal staff would be in attendance and ready for an all-night session. At 10.30 or 11 o'clock Mr. Churchill would settle down to a final revision of what he had prepared, and as the various sections were completed they would come out to us for putting into Speech Form, already mentioned. We knew it was no use starting off in a hurry; the night was before us, and we would type steadily and carefully, seldom speaking. For speeches we used a special octavo sheet, and made four or five carbon copies. Speech Form would look like this:

> We cannot yet see how deliverance will come
>   or when it will come,

> but nothing is more certain
> > than tt every trace of Hitler's footsteps,
>
> every stain of his infected
> > and corroding fingers,
>
> will be sponged and purged
> > and, if need be, blasted
> > > fr the surface of the earth.

At 2 o'clock or so the Prime Minister would go to bed, leaving the balance of the script ready for us. I used to try to send Mrs. Hill off to bed, too, knowing she would have to be up in good time for morning duty. Then I would plod steadily on. I used to find about 2.30 I became intolerably sleepy and felt low in energy, but about 4.30 my spirits seemed to revive; perhaps the early morning breeze was refreshing, and I would feel full of strength again. Usually one finished about 5 o'clock, then one sorted out the copies to make the five or six complete sets, "klopped" the top copy in the lower left-hand corner and placed a long tag through the holes, put this copy on a chair outside the Prime Minister's bedroom so that it could be taken in to him immediately he woke—undressed and tottered in one's housecoat down the twirly, draughty stairs for two to three hours' sleep, it being by this time almost 6 o'clock.

But one's troubles were not yet over. By 10 o'clock one would be dressed again (feeling perhaps just a trifle snappish), breakfasted and ready for last-minute alterations. Invariably there would be a big flap on: it was in the character of the man and impossible to avoid—it *always* happened. Often during the night he would have had a new idea and Mrs. Hill would have typed several pages. The Private Secretaries would be hastily checking this with the Departments concerned, and then one would receive it for last-minute putting into Speech Form. Then some of the finished copy would be altered—the alterations put hastily in with Mr. Churchill's red pen, usually quite unreadable as, being still human, he would be getting worked up for the effort—and these pages would need recopying. As one was poring over the red squiggles, not wishing to have to go in and ask, the news would come through, via Sawyers, "He's gone for his bath", and the last-stretch gallop would begin. No time to feel tired—just get it done. And, of course, one way or another, it always was done.

Afterwards one would feel anxious in case, in haste, one had arranged the pages in the wrong order, or put a "now" instead of a "not" which would not be noticed until the P.M. spoke. I do not think in fact there was ever an occasion when this did happen, but in any case I think Mr. Churchill would easily have surmounted such errors.

And then, at the moment when he was supposed to leave, when the car and driver stood outside and the Private Secretary on duty stood waiting, holding the final script, he would emerge from his bedroom looking fresh and beautifully groomed in his black coat and striped trousers, often with a rosebud in his buttonhole, and accompanied by Mrs. Churchill. We would stand at the office doorway to see him off, and usually he would have a beaming smile and a word of thanks for us, which inspired the most furious feelings of devotion and loyalty.

Sometimes, however, things did not run so smoothly. Perhaps a shorter statement would be contemplated and there would not be the urgent necessity for advance preparation. There was always something in the Prime Minister that reacted well to an emergency and a last-minute rush, so much so that sometimes one almost felt he did it on purpose. Perhaps in the days beforehand he would not be in the mood for dictating the particular subject on which he was to speak, or perhaps he would try for some hours and the words would flow like treacle on a cold day—and as the time for the speech drew near it would be hardly more than begun. And of course, too, sometimes an unexpected event would call for an immediate statement, with only an hour or so to prepare it. In these cases there would be a terrible crisis on the morning in question, we would all look tense, and later on Mrs. Hill and I would go with the Prime Minister to his room in the House of Commons, there to complete the Speech Form before he went to the Chamber. The anxiety and haste can well be imagined. The Private Secretaries on duty would stand sympathetically around, at times doing the checking and "klopping" and "tagging" themselves, as Big Ben chimed the passing quarters. In extreme cases one took down from the Prime Minister straight into Speech Form on the typewriter, which always seemed rather a responsibility.

When these flaps were over, one would feel completely fagged out. Luckily the third on our staff would be there to do late duty that night, and I, for one, would stagger off home with my little suitcase and, having asked my friends to excuse my unsociability, would sleep until 8.30 the following morning.

◆ ◆ ◆

I often wondered to myself, in the period before beginning to work for Mr. Churchill personally, what is a Great Man like? Will he seem different from other people? There are, of course, other Great Men in the world, but in Mr.

Churchill's case I think the answer was definitely Yes. One was at once aware of the great force at his command, of the strength and determination within him, of the vast stores of knowledge his head contained. To me he stood head and shoulders above the others. No one could doubt his utter single-mindedness and nobility of purpose. He never failed to uphold the Right.

He was, of course, in possession of boundless self-confidence—without it he could never have been the man he was—and his background (combined with the British caste system) made him a person who expected to be approached with great respect by those who worked for him. He was careful to keep each stratum in its proper place. I cannot imagine, for instance, that he was ever troubled with cheeky servants or secretaries—no one would have dared—but at the same time he always remembered to respect the position of each one of us. He might order his valet about; to us he said "Please", or "Would you".

He always concentrated upon that which was important, and was able to discount that which was merely tiresome. I am sure this was true of his prosecution of the war; in our sphere we noticed it in a less general sense. For instance, the Annexe flat was, as I have said, not ideally situated for the Churchills' use, in that it was also a passage through to the office of the No.10 official staff, and visitors arriving early for an appointment with the Prime Minister and being marched through to wait in the Private Secretaries' office would occasionally be astonished to be confronted by a figure enveloped in an enormous white bath towel crossing back to the bedroom from the bathroom. No one really *likes* being caught in a bath towel. But Mr. Churchill was always equal to these moments, and the visitor would be put at his ease by a stately greeting from the towel-clad figure.

In October of that first year of my time with him, Mr. Churchill visited Harrow, his old school, and talked to the boys. One thing he told them was "Never, never, never, never give in"—which was like him. When they sang their school song, there was a verse added in honour of their Old Boy. It began like this:

> *Not less we praise in darker days*
> *The Leader of our Nation,*
> *And Churchill's name shall win acclaim*
> *From each new generation.*

But he asked that the word "darker" should be altered to "sterner": he said they were not dark days, they were great days. That was also like him.

Once one was used to working for the Prime Minister, working for his colleagues held no terrors whatsoever. Beside his full-blooded confidence they seemed pale. I was often "lent" to the Foreign Secretary, or Lord Beaverbrook, or General Smuts, or anyone who happened to be visiting Mr. Churchill and wished to put something on paper, and I soon realized that the job I was fitting into was something quite different and far more difficult than it would have been with any other man. Far more interesting and rewarding, too.

Of the many, many speeches, statements and broadcasts he made in those years, I still think particularly of one of the first in which I took any part, which made me think, "This man is different." This was a speech broadcast in June 1941 to Rochester University, New York, from which he had just received an Honorary Doctorate of Law. I still have some pages of the original draft, dictated in the Cabinet Room—much altered in his handwriting—in which, speaking of the necessity to fight the evil forces of Nazism and the awakening of this realization in America, he said:

'The world is witnessing the birth throes of a sublime resolve. I shall presume to confess to you that I have no doubts what that resolve will be.

'The destiny of mankind is not decided by material computation. When great causes are on the move in the world, stirring all men's souls, drawing them from their firesides, casting aside comfort, wealth and the pursuit of happiness in response to impulses at once awe-striking and irresistible, we learn that we are spirits, not animals, and that something is going on in space and time, and beyond space and time, which, whether we like it or not, spells Duty.'

It is not my plan to make any further quotations from Mr. Churchill's speeches, which are all written down elsewhere. But perhaps I may be allowed this one.

There was that in Mr. Churchill's make-up which made his dictation seem exciting and colourful—his sense of destiny and a realization of the historic nature of his documents and decisions. As he dictated he would try out various adjectives to himself, and would invariably produce something striking. "A cacophonous chorus"—how on earth did one write that in shorthand? "Prodigious efforts are required"—quite right, they always were. "That dark day"—when Tobruk fell, with a shake of his head and a thickening of his voice. "A noble sight"—a convoy of eighty British merchant ships. "The clashing, joyous peals" of the church bells which rang to celebrate the victory at Alamein. "The jaws of the Russian winter" which closed on the German armies. And, speaking of the vicissitudes of the war, "The waves dash over us, the currents swirl around us, but the tide bears us forward with its broad, resistless flood." One could go on like this for a long time.

And just to add to the excitement of life, very often his documents were drafted late at night, past midnight, in a frantic rush of urgency. As he reached the peroration his voice would rise to a roar, or sink to a husky whisper, according to what he said. And then one would be more or less told, "Go and type for your life."

But perhaps the quality in Mr. Churchill's make-up that endeared him particularly to his staff was something quite different—a complete unselfconsciousness in certain respects, something almost naïve, an ability to be accidentally funny, as it were. The atmosphere of tension and anxiety in the office, which was a natural result of the state of the war, was frequently broken by silly events arising from this quality—which happenings we always welcomed because they made us giggle and kept us from becoming too serious about life. The following incident gave us all pleasure.

One night the Prime Minister decided to go to the roof of the Annexe building to watch an air raid which was taking place. He did this sometimes, despite all persuasion to the contrary. The night was cold, but wrapped in his coat he found a comfortable seat on the roof and professed himself warm. His companions became anxious for his welfare, but there he remained. Suddenly the party was dispersed by the arrival of a somewhat bothered officer from the lower regions, who reported that downstairs the place was full of smoke, they could none of them work—and would the P.M. please mind not sitting any longer on the chimney, where he had unknowingly perched himself. No wonder he felt nice and warm!

Another evening he was sitting in his study with one or two advisers, working on his Box. I had incurred his wrath for a silly typing mistake, but was not upset about it. However, having a slight cold, I ventured some minutes later to blow my nose quietly, and he noticed and thought I was crying. "Good Heavens," he said, "you mustn't mind me. We're all toads beneath the harrow, you know." In a few minutes he dictated a very short note indeed, as follows:

> FIRST SEA LORD.
> I am in general agreement with this proposal.

When I handed it to him for initialling he said, "Oh, very good indeed, very well typed, how quick you were." General Ismay was never able to forget that incident.

Different?—yes, he certainly was different. You, I am sure, have a deep admiration for Sir Winston Churchill. I *know* that another such personality does not exist.

6

The weekly exit to Chequers was an important part of our routine. The weekend was not really a time to relax. Many jobs were put by for those days and many official guests were entertained, both for the information they could give the Prime Minister and by way of compliment to visitors from overseas or to those who had performed some particular service (such as Guy Gibson, V.C., the Dambuster).

Chequers is a delightful country house which was given to the nation by Lord and Lady Lee of Fareham in 1921 as a place of rest and recreation for the current Prime Minister. It is full of beautiful things—paintings, antique furniture, books, ornaments and so on—and can boast a secret staircase to a room on the second floor, the Prison Room, where long ago Lady Mary Grey, sister of Lady Jane, was kept prisoner for two years by Queen Elizabeth I. It was a drive of approximately an hour, if you wasted no time. The route lay down the Notting Hill High Street, past the White City, on past Northolt aerodrome, through Amersham and Gerrard's Cross and so to Chequers, guarded in those days by a detachment of the Coldstream Guards.

Leaving for Chequers on a Friday afternoon was always quite a performance. The Prime Minister would give a time—perhaps he would say, "We'll leave at 3.30 and I'll have my rest when we get there." At 3.15, therefore, the three big black cars would be at the garden gate of No.10 with their drivers in readiness, the third car loaded up with two telephone operators and Sawyers. Waiting inside the office would be the Private Secretary on duty at Chequers that weekend (another remained on duty at the Annexe), the Naval Aide, Commander Thompson, two of the Personal Secretaries and two detectives (they were allocated to the Prime Minister by Scotland Yard and went wherever he did). Perhaps at 4 o'clock the third car, unable to wait longer, would leave. Time would pass, the buzzer would sound, telephone calls would be put through from the Cabinet Room, or perhaps Mr. Churchill would decide to see one of his advisers before leaving. Or perhaps an urgent telegram would come in and have to be dealt with on the spot.

Perhaps at 5.30 he would decide to have his rest in town and leave for Chequers at 7 o'clock after all. Then all would relax and resume other work. Later the vigil would be renewed, and probably about 7.35, when one had almost given up hope of ever getting away, he would step quickly from the Cabinet Room with a twinkle in his eye and a look of "Hurray, we're off"; would be helped into his coat by one messenger, take his hat, stick and gloves from another, and be down the back stairs and out through the garden in a few seconds, while a panting train of staff hastily grabbed boxes, books and pencils, and hurried to reach each his allotted place before the general circus left.

The Prime Minister's time was too valuable for him to waste the hour of the journey, and unless there was a visitor of importance with whom he wished to speak, who could suitably be asked to ride with him, one of the personal staff would sit beside him and he would work in the normal manner. Large jobs, such as speeches or broadcasts, or reports to the President, would be kept for the journey to Chequers. Mr. Churchill did not care for slow travel, and would congratulate the driver when he managed to do the hour's trip in fifty minutes. It did not make it easier to get down all he said, however, when the car rocked and swayed through the outskirts of London, jumping traffic-lights and driving to the right of traffic islands, police bell sounding. There was the usual feeling of haste, of winding up the clock. One would sit with book balanced on one knee, scribbling hard, one's left hand holding spare pencils, his glasses' case or an extra cigar, sometimes with one's foot keeping open his precious Box, which otherwise would have slammed shut as we swung round a corner. There was a small light to shine on one's book when it became dark. We usually arrived just in time for dinner at 8.30, and then there would be a scramble to get everything typed before he began work again.

Sometimes Mr. Churchill would decide to have his afternoon rest during the journey, and then he would place over his eyes a round black bandage which Sawyers always kept in his overcoat pocket. On these occasions he would invite Commander Thompson to travel in the car with him, and after a short time he would put on his black bandage and sit sleeping in the corner. One Friday afternoon a quaint little incident occurred.

Commander Thompson had a slight cough, and knowing how little Mr. Churchill liked such ailments he purchased a bottle of gargle, which he put into his coat pocket. When he heard that he was to travel with the Prime Minister that afternoon to Chequers he hastily went out and bought a bottle of soothing throat syrup, so that he would not annoy him by coughing. But alas, as the Prime Minister sat peacefully sleeping during the drive, Commander Thompson, feeling a tickle coming in his throat, reached into the wrong pocket and swallowed a good dose of the gargle by mistake. He was shaken with a tremendous fit of coughing, which woke Mr. Churchill. The car was stopped and I was fished out of the following car to change places with poor Commander Thompson because, Mr. Churchill said, "Tommy seems to have a very bad cough." Afterwards we teased him about it plenty.

At Chequers we lived in moderate comfort, waited on by the household staff. But we needed that comfort, for we invariably worked flat out all weekend. Bed for the late shift would seldom be before 3 o'clock, and we would be busy all day too. The house was always full of visitors—business visitors. All the well-known personalities of the war came there, sometimes only for a meal but usually for one or two nights. Our own Cabinet Ministers and Service Chiefs would be represented each weekend, and we frequently saw visitors such as Mr. Harry Hopkins, Mr. Winant and Mr. Harriman; later, Generals Eisenhower and Marshall and Clark; Mr. Mackenzie King; Sir Earle Page and Mr. Casey, the Australians; General Smuts; General de Gaulle; General Sikorski; and many others too numerous to mention. The Americans found the house cold; poor Mr. Hopkins, who was thin, always grumbled at the lack of central heating and usually stated on arrival, "I brought plenty of long woollen underwear this time." General Smuts obviously enjoyed the country atmosphere, but disliked the extraordinary hours, being used to rising at 6 o'clock and retiring at 9 o'clock. He was a great favourite with us all—the Prime Minister was always glad to see him and listened to what he had to say, and he always had a kind smile of recognition for the staff.

After going to Chequers regularly for some months I felt quite at home in the household and could concentrate on work without anxiety. In the evenings Mr. Churchill would often sit in the office, beside the cheerful fire there, and talk to General Ismay about the most dreadful secrets of the war—Future Operations! Mostly they would use the code-names for places or particular plans—shades of the Secret Service! One evening during such a chat the Prime Minister was dictating about a possible descent upon the island of Rhodes in the Aegean Sea; I knew it was this, because once or twice the name Rhodes slipped out by mistake. Presently he swung round on me, saying with a twinkle, "Miss Layton, you are the repository of the nation's secrets." I was a bit flummoxed and could only say, "But I won't tell," whereat he answered, "I know you won't—I know you'd rather die"—which was true.

I grew to love the office at Chequers. Sitting at the desk, one looked out through a latticed window into the front courtyard, where we drove in. It was brick-walled, and in the centre was a graceful figure, a statue of the goddess Hygeia, I was told. In summer the sun would pour in, the iris and poppies in the beds outside would give a brilliant touch of colour, and away in the woods beyond the front gate a cuckoo would be shouting his head off. If it were possible anywhere, one forgot the war there for a little, while Mr. Churchill slept late in the morning as sometimes he did.

The central chamber at Chequers, around which the rest of the house was built, was called the Great Hall. It was two stories high, with many wonderful paintings on the walls, and along one side halfway up ran a gallery, off which most of the bedrooms opened. One could stand there unobserved and watch the company below. One weekend a visitor was M. Benno Moiseiwitsch, the famed pianist, who had been working ceaselessly for the Red Cross "Aid to Russia" Fund, which Mrs. Churchill was sponsoring and giving a great deal of time to. From the gallery we listened to him playing, on the grand piano below, the well-known Ballade of Chopin, which was a favourite of the Prime Minister's. I think he played it several times that weekend, and a little later on there arrived a most beautiful present for Mr. Churchill, a bronze statuette of a Russian horseman, an antique, around the base of which had been newly carved the opening notes of the Ballade. How I loved hearing M. Moiseiwitsch play, and how I admired that statuette

The second principal room of the house was named the Hawtrey Room after a former owner of Chequers. It also was full of antique furniture and beautiful objects. Here were composed many, many of the Prime Minister's speeches and broadcasts. It was his favourite spot at Chequers for dictating anything lengthy, and to me it was very wonderful to sit in that room, where I loved the pictures and portraits and the lovely old furniture, and take down the words which would, I knew, be the talk of the whole nation within a day or so. Perhaps I made too much of this; the others used to laugh at me sometimes. But, as I say, to me it seemed very wonderful.

We would have a film show almost every night after dinner, arranged by the Ministry of Information, in the Long Gallery which was on the first floor above the Hawtrey Room. One night it was "Dangerous Moonlight"—about the bombing of Poland—but in the middle Mr. Churchill felt he must get on with a statement he had to dictate. So we left the film and went below, and soon he was pacing the Hawtrey Room, and the words were rolling out, telling the House of Commons that to the original programme he had promised them of blood, toil, tears and sweat must now be added "many shortcomings, mistakes and disappointments". At the same time the chords of the Warsaw Concerto came rumbling down from upstairs, seeming to heighten the drama I was witnessing.

Mr. Churchill would frequently broadcast to the nation on a Sunday night immediately before the 9 o'clock news. This would almost always be done from

Chequers, which was suitably wired. B.B.C. men would arrive during the day, and when the moment came in the evening, we would sit in the Curator's room, quite near the room from which he was speaking, checking his words by the script as we listened to the broadcast emanating from London. Broadcast Form was much like Speech Form, only done on quarto paper with much longer lines. A broadcast always meant a particularly busy weekend.

A most important part of our work at Chequers was keeping the Prime Minister up to date with the latest reports of the war received at the Annexe. There was a device attached to our telephones called the Scrambler, by which one could speak in complete secrecy to someone on another Scrambling telephone. By pressing a button one "went over to Secret" or Scrambled, and when the business was completed one pressed another button, which returned the line to normal. As soon as any news was received for the Prime Minister by the Private Secretary on duty at the Annexe—he would ring through on the direct line to Chequers—one of us would be summoned to the telephone with book and pencil; we would go over to Secret, and the telegram or whatever it was would be dictated by the Private Secretary, to be typed out at full speed at our end. In particularly urgent cases one would first read the document over to the Prime Minister from one's notebook, and woe betide her whose outlines failed to register at first glance. I used to find when taking down something vital I would be so concentrated upon writing correctly that at the end I would have little idea of what had been said, and could hardly tell the anxious and impatient audience whether the battle had been lost or won until I had read through my Pitman's best.

As mentioned before, we would also frequently be lent to Mr. Churchill's guests for a spot of work. I was temporarily bowled over by the charm of Lord Halifax, on a visit from Washington where he was Ambassador, for whom I did some typing—at which the others sniggered. Frequently the American visitors would need help; Mr. Harry Hopkins, for instance, gave what was called the Postscript to the News on the B.B.C. one Sunday night, and I had to do the fifteen pages of script several times. The Americans were always extremely polite and full of apologies for taking up our time. Actually we found working for them something of a rest-cure, for they seemed quite surprised that we usually got it right the first time. General Ismay, of course, always had lots of jobs for us. General Smuts sometimes dictated. Luckily we had good food at Chequers, which kept us going; extra rations were allowed for the official entertaining, and there was a farm connected with the estate, which helped.

General Sir Hastings Ismay, who was Mr. Churchill's close associate and liaison officer between him and Service Chiefs, being Secretary to the Chiefs of Staff

Committee, was at Chequers most weekends. He was a charming person, always full of fun, and far more approachable than most of the British officers. Sometimes before dinner he would bring glasses of sherry into the office for the personal staff—amid many giggles—and, somehow, having to drink it rather hastily without being caught at it made it seem all the more delicious. I always felt his chief cleverness lay in knowing just how to treat the Prime Minister; how to bring him round to a necessary decision which he didn't like, how to break bad news to him, how to get his agreement when the Chiefs of Staff most wanted it. General Ismay's contribution to the smooth running of our lives was enormous.

Another frequent visitor to Chequers whom we all knew very well was Lord Cherwell, the Prime Minister's old friend and scientific adviser. He was a quiet, unassuming man, tall, with a quiet voice and a hesitant way of speaking; a bachelor and a vegetarian, the last man you'd call a fire-eater. But his knowledge was vast; he had figures and statistics at his fingertips and was able to produce at short notice any data the P.M. required. I expect the word for him would be "brilliant"; to us in the office he was one of the gentlest and friendliest among Mr. Churchill's circle.

It was a great moment for me when, after being some months in the office, I was allowed by Mrs. Hill to take a turn at travelling in the car with the Prime Minister on the way up from Chequers. And I certainly picked a fine morning for my debut. In November every year, Lord Mayor's Day is celebrated in the City of London, and on this occasion it is customary for the Prime Minister to be the guest of honour and speaker. During the war this celebration took the form of a civic luncheon. This yearly speech is regarded as an important statement of Government policy. It so happened that on this Monday—it was the 10th November, 1941—Mr. Churchill was to attend the Lord Mayor's Day Luncheon, and so far he had not had time to begin on the preparation of his speech, which, it being a public affair, had to be checked by the Departments concerned before delivery (for instance, if he spoke about the Army, the War Office would be asked for confirmation; about security measures, the Home Office, and so on). He planned to leave Chequers early, dictating it in the car, but as often happened he dilly-dallied and it was 10.30 before he finally stepped into the car and sat down beside me. I was feeling somewhat on tenterhooks. We roared off on our way, and for a while he sat in silence. Then his hand began to gesture, and I knew it was coming. But, Good Heavens, I couldn't catch a word of the first phrase, and sat stiff with fright, remembering the sound as I wrote automatically what followed. At last I sighed with relief—it must have been "Alike in times of peace and war". By the time we reached No.10 the greater part was down on paper, at any rate. But it was now 11.30, and at 12.30 he had to leave for the City. As we arrived at the garden gate he said, "Now run inside and type like HELL."

I did, putting it into Speech Form, but presently there was an interruption. "Go into the Cabinet Room with your book, the Prime Minister wants Mr. Eden to hear that bit that has a bearing on Foreign Affairs." I went in, scruffing hastily through the pages of my notebook, and sat down. "Now, Miss Layton," said Mr. Churchill with a twinkle, "I want you to read that bit to the Foreign Secretary. Not too fast and not too slow: not too loud and not too soft." Luckily for me, I found the place. It happened quite often that the Prime Minister would ask one to read back his dictation to a roomful of his colleagues, so that one became used to rather a select audience and to being mighty careful with one's outlines.

Of course the speech was finished and checked in time—*just* in time—and he arrived safely at the luncheon—just in time.

Chequers was, as I have said, guarded day and night by the Coldstream Guards, and there was a roof-spotter always on the lookout for raiding aircraft; but the Germans, we heard, had vowed to "get Churchill", and therefore when the moon was full and they were apt to come over in force we did not go to Chequers for the weekend but to "the other place", a heavily guarded secret. It was Dytchley Park, the home of Mr. and Mrs. Ronald Tree, old friends of the Churchills, and was not far from Blenheim Palace (where Mr. Churchill was born on the 30th November, 1874). It was a journey of about two hours from London. I only went there once or twice, as soon after my advent the danger from raiding decreased. Coming from Canada I found this huge Georgian palace of a country house quite overwhelming; there seemed to be so many butlers and footmen around, the old family-retainer types; the front hall was as big as a cinema, and the honoured guests all slept in swanky four-poster beds with drapes. I was particularly impressed by the lavender bags which were placed in the little baskets of paper in all the bathrooms—a refined touch!

My first impressions of Dytchley Park were perhaps a little damped by the remembrance of my first morning there, when I had sat behind the typewriter near the biggest and swankiest four-poster bed. Mr. Churchill had been dictating something about Ceylon, and had mentioned the naval base Trincomalee. Unfortunately I had never heard of it, and I wrote a horrid-looking word beginning "Chink …". When I handed the document over there was a short pause, then the storm broke. "Where on earth were you educated? Haven't you ever heard of TRINCOMALEE? Why don't you learn some geography? Why don't you read some books? …" etc.,etc.

But that was in the bad old days, at the beginning.

At other times Mr. Churchill would decide that he really must have a sight of his dear deserted house in Kent, Chartwell. The big house was, of course, closed up, but Chartwell Cottage, which he built with his own hands in the days when he was out of office, was constantly occupied by a relation. If he decided to stay overnight, Mr. and Mrs. Churchill, the Private Secretary, Sawyers and Mrs. Landemare the cook would be housed there with a squeeze, poor Commander Thompson would be left in London, Mrs. Hill and the two detectives would put up in the nearby village of Westerham, and I, being on late duty, would be left at the big house to fend for myself.

I well remember the first of such occasions, when I was still new and anxious. Mr. Churchill's study in the big house—it was an ancient room with a high, arched ceiling, formerly a chapel—had been opened up for him, and we therefore opened the office also, dust-covered as it was. There was a complicated telephone extension system, and a sudden loud buzzer to indicate one's presence was required. Few of the lights were in operation, and the dark rooms and passages were filled with sheet-swathed pieces of furniture. In addition, there was the fact that there would be no one to fall back on if I had a bad session of dictation, and when Mrs. Hill left for the village at dinnertime I felt distinctly nervous. However, all passed off well that evening, and when bed was announced and Mr. Churchill and the Private Secretary left for the cottage, I retired to a bed which had been left by chance in the dining-room, where, it being a warm summer night, I merely climbed under the dustsheet that covered it and slept.

In the morning I was awakened by footsteps and the dragging of a dressing-gown cord. I looked up quickly—the sun was shining, and there stood Mr. Churchill in gown and huge-brimmed hat, going the rounds of his loved home by daylight. He looked astonished, then grinned broadly and said "Hullo..." and walked out. Later I overheard him telling Mrs. Churchill, "I went into the dining-room and there she was, asleep, fast asleep in bed."

One grew to be very fond of Chartwell and its surroundings. The banks of rhododendrons were splashes of colour in the late spring and summer, and the magnolia tree had the hugest white blooms you ever saw. The trees and grassy paths, overgrown as they then were, had an air of peace and content in those days of toil, and the lake at the bottom of the hill, the home in those days of Mr. Churchill's black swans, made an attractive picture. It was typical of Mr. Churchill, ever loyal as he was to his family, his friends, colleagues and those who worked for him, that he should have been deeply and permanently attached to his home.

7

But, it may well be asked, what about the war? What was happening all this time I was getting used to the routine of the Prime Minister's life?

Shortly after I joined Mr. Churchill's staff, an event of first importance took place—Germany attacked Russia. He called it the "Fourth Climacteric" (trust him to find a word no one else had ever heard of), the others being the fall of France, the Battle of Britain and the passing of Lease-Lend. And now we were no longer fighting alone. That fact was a comfort, even though things were not going well for ourselves or the Russians. Telegrams began to pass between the Prime Minister and Marshal Stalin—Uncle Joe, as we called him in the office, and later on merely U.J.

Then there was the Atlantic Meeting, which thrilled the world with its unexpectedness and its promise of co-operation between the peace-loving nations.

And then, on the 7th December, 1941, Pearl Harbour and the following day the British declaration of war against Japan. We were now three Great Powers fighting together, and that was very different from standing alone against the armed might of Germany. The exchange of telegrams between the "Former Naval Person" and the President grew enormously in volume, "Former Naval Person" being a later stage of "Naval Person", with which name Mr. Churchill had signed his telegrams to the President when he was First Lord of the Admiralty.

So that 1941, while it was a hard year full of struggle and disappointment, at least ended with ourselves in a far better position than at its outset. 1942 was to prove a very different sort of year, the first eight months being probably the most discouraging of the war, seemingly a succession of setbacks, disappointments and failures, with lack of unanimity at home to add to its other trials; and towards the end of the year, the turning of the tide.

The Prime Minister's mind was fully engaged with both aspects of his double task—being First Minister of the Crown and also Minister of Defence. He was in top gear on both counts, as it were. Much of his time was taken up with War Cabinet and Cabinet meetings on the one hand, and meetings with the Chiefs of Staff on the other. I will not try to guess at the power he wielded among them; I was naturally not present at any of these meetings. Cabinet Ministers usually addressed him on formal occasions as Mr. Prime Minister; Service Chiefs called him Prime Minister or Sir—to which latter I do not think he objected, though he did not like to be called Sir by a civilian.

To me it was interesting to note the difference in response between the Cabinet Ministers and Service Chiefs when he interviewed them. The former seemed full of eloquent language, and anxious to gain their point by diplomatic presentation of their case. The latter could be surprisingly gruff at times and would only expound their subject when invited to do so. Ministers like Mr. Eden, Mr. Oliver Lyttelton and Sir John Anderson would sometimes stop to pass a few moments in friendly conversation with the staff, this being according to their upbringing. The Chiefs of Staff almost never spoke to one, such was their sincere devotion to duty and their desire not to waste time.

When I first arrived in the office I was mystified by the term "Chiefs of Staff", which played such an important part in our lives. It seemed that at least half the Prime Minister's Minutes and directives were addressed to them—C.O.S., or C.O.S. Committee, or General Ismay for C.O.S. I soon found out that they were the heads of the three Armed Services and together the head of all the British forces. The Naval Chief, the First Sea Lord (or 1 S.L. when Mr. Churchill was in a hurry), was at that time Admiral Sir Dudley Pound, a gallant figure in the British Naval tradition; the head of the Army, the Chief of the Imperial General Staff or C.I.G.S., was General Sir Alan Brooke, a man of exceptional intelligence—we saw him almost every day; and the Chief of the Air Staff, the C.A.S., was Air Marshal Sir Charles Portal, a tall, striking-looking man, one of the most successful of the war leaders and highly thought of by everyone, but a man who shunned publicity for himself.

And here let me mention another figure—the Chief of Combined Operations, or C.C.O., whose appointment was made towards the end of 1941 as thoughts started turning to the eventual landings in France. This was Admiral Lord Louis Mountbatten, who came to greater and greater prominence as the war progressed. I suppose he ranked next after the Chiefs of Staff. Later in the war he became Supreme Commander of the South-East Asia Command. His was quite the most glamorous personality among our circles; not only was he tall and extremely good-looking, with gold braid flashing on his uniform, but he seemed to exude a special kind of charm which had us all falling over backwards. Certainly he had much to be proud of, for his men adored him and would have followed him to the death.

Sir Alan Brooke was a frequent visitor, and often he would be shown into the bedroom in the morning for a brief consultation. On these occasions, of course, the Personal Secretary would leave the room. The C.I.G.S. always appeared to me something of an enigma; he seemed so calm and well controlled, and yet the expression of his face sometimes betokened that he had strong feelings beneath the surface—feelings not always in accord with those of the man to whom he was responsible. We all knew the Prime Minister thought very highly of his capabilities, but merely to see him from the angle from which we viewed him one would not have put him down as a Great Man.

One morning the Prime Minister was talking on the telephone to Brookie, when the following scene, of which I was the sole spectator, occurred. But first let me explain.

Mr. Churchill was very fond of cats, and at this time the kitchen staff acquired a young Persian, grey and fluffy, whom they named Smokey. This little animal became much attached to the P.M., who returned his affection. Every morning as breakfast was taken in Smokey would be at the door waiting to be let in too; he would sit on the bed and receive graciously any small piece of meat, or perhaps a little milk, and then he would sleep for hours on the bed while the Prime Minister worked, sometimes covering him accidentally with a Top Secret report. Unfortunately, as Smokey grew up he became more and more wild and ill-behaved, till he was a positive menace to anyone entering the room. Legs and stockings were his speciality. One never liked to make a fuss when ladders and even blood appeared, but privately Smokey was called by some uncomplimentary and unrepeatable names.

On the morning in question Mr. Churchill sat in bed and Smokey sat on the blankets watching him. The Prime Minister's telephone conversation with the C.I.G.S. was long and anxious; his thoughts were far away; his toes wiggled under the blankets. I saw Smokey's tail switch as he watched, and wondered what was going to happen. Suddenly he pounced on the toes and bit hard. It must have hurt, for Mr. Churchill, startled, kicked him right into the corner of the room shouting "Get off, you fool" into the telephone. Then he remembered. "Oh," he said, "I didn't mean you," and then seeing Smokey looking somewhat dazed in the corner, "Poor little thing." Confusion was complete, the C.I.G.S. hung up hastily and telephoned the Private Secretary to know what was happening. It took a long time to get it all sorted out, and Sir Alan Brooke assured that it was not his fault.

Another visitor who quite often came to see the Prime Minister in bed during the morning was the officer in charge of the Intelligence Section, a gentleman who went by the intriguing name of "C". Intelligence reports would be sent in to the Prime Minister as they were received, but when there was something of particular importance "C" would come along himself to deliver the news. It was some time before I saw "C". I heard about him, of course, and was told that if he was shown into the room I must not display signs of curiosity by dallying, as he would be sure to have some awful and weighty secret to impart. When at last I came face to face with him I was surprised to find he looked pleasantly ordinary, and not at all like the secretive and piercing-eyed "C" of my imagination.

When there was news of a calamity, Mr. Churchill was always the fountain of strength from which emanated comfort and reassurance. But within himself he minded—*terribly*. He is a patriot to his last ounce, he loves the British nation; and when lives or prestige were lost it hurt him deeply. One of the most terrible blows of the war for him was no doubt the sinking of the battleship *Prince of Wales* (in which he had gone to the Atlantic Meeting) and the battlecruiser *Repulse* by the Japanese in December 1941. Always a lover of things naval, that was to him a personal loss as well as a loss to our naval forces and prestige. When a city had received a bad bombing, he would try whenever possible to pay it a visit, to cheer up the inhabitants, but his grief at the sight of the devastation was moving to see. However, he was always on top of his feelings, and the people, revitalized, would show their delight at the sight of him. Once or twice I went with him in London to see bomb scars, sometimes only a short time after the bombs had fallen. On one occasion I remember him speaking to the shaken occupants of a recently shattered small home. As he left, some papers blew about, so he turned to say quickly "Hope that's the Income Tax form", which left them smiling.

He was keen, too, to keep his own eye on those concerned with the air-raid warning system and other forms of civil defence, always with an idea that there might be an invasion from the Continent. Any suggestion of lethargy or inefficiency which came to his eye would be swiftly and angrily investigated. On occasions he would like to turn up unexpectedly somewhere, to see for himself how things were running.

An instance of this was our sudden descent on the Northolt aerodrome one Monday morning on our return journey from Chequers to London. I always watched out for the airfield as we passed it, intrigued by the strange camouflage markings across its centre which I was told gave it the appearance from the air of a green field crossed by a stream. This morning, to my surprise, the cars turned off from the main route (the Prime Minister was accompanied in his car by the Chief of the Air Staff) and swept past an anxious guard into the airfield's enclosure. The Station Commandant was requested to sound the Emergency signal, and quite soon men were running about in all directions, looking somewhat alarmed. Mr. Churchill was not altogether satisfied with the reaction and, stepping once more into his car, directed the driver to drive around the field. Some distance away he came upon a small canteen standing by itself, displaying no activity. He hopped out and strode quickly through the front door. A few moments later three or four very bothered-looking men emerged at the trot, one hastily grabbing a rifle from somewhere. I couldn't help laughing to myself to think how one would feel if one were sitting in all innocence drinking a cup of morning coffee, and suddenly the door opened and in marched a furious Prime Minister, particularly if it were Winston Churchill and his fury were directed at oneself.

Towards the end of 1941 the northern cities of England received a pasting from the German bombers, and the Prime Minister decided to make a tour of a few days to view the damage and encourage the people. It so happened that Mrs. Hill, who had a son of school age, had planned to take a weekend off in order to attend one of his school functions—she saw so little of him—and the trip arranged was to end only on the Sunday morning. Therefore she put a note into the Personal file in the P.M.'s box, asking if I might accompany him on the trip instead of herself. For several days he did not see it, and I was alternately hopeful and despairing, for of course I *longed* to go. At last, only the day before he was leaving, he saw it and wrote Yes.

The Prime Minister would go off by train every few months to tour some part of Britain, and from that time onward I was allowed to accompany him more often than not, as Mrs. Hill was not very keen on going. I adored every minute of it. General Ismay would invariably go with the P.M. if there were any military installations to be visited by the way—which was usually the case—and visiting Ministers or Generals from other countries were sometimes taken along as a compliment and to give Mr. Churchill an opportunity of personal discussions during the evenings, which would be spent on the train. Dr. Evatt, Sir Earle Page and Mr. Richard Casey were some of these; General Smuts, Mr. Mackenzie King, General Marshall and Mr. Hopkins all accompanied us on train trips at some time or other. A Private Secretary was always on duty, also Commander Thompson, Sawyers, the detectives and the official photographers.

Our special train would usually leave one of the main London stations between 12 and 1 o'clock in the morning (giving us all, according to Mr. Churchill, the chance of a nice early night). It consisted of the Prime Minister's special coach, which contained his bedroom, bathroom and lounge, and the office; a dining-car divided into two sections, for the main party and for the staff;

and a first-class sleeping coach with twelve compartments, on whose doors would be tickets denoting the allotted occupant.

The routine for me would be that on arising I would telephone through to the Annexe for the morning news. The Scrambling telephone would have been connected to the nearest exchange as soon as we arrived at the outlying station where we were "stabling" for the rest of the night, and by mentioning the magic number Rapid Falls 4466 one would be through to the No.10 exchange, from any part of England, usually within a minute or so. Then perhaps the Prime Minister would work on his Box, after which the train would be drawn into the main station at the arranged time, and the party would go off about its business, the Prime Minister in the van and the photographers in the rear, leaving Sawyers and me to mind the train and have all in readiness for their return, including any news or information from London.

On this particular occasion he toured Newcastle, Hull and Sheffield, and received a tumultuous welcome from the assembled crowds. He spoke in each case from the Town Hall through a microphone. The bombing had been cruel, and while I would never say that morale was low, it was certainly raised by a visit from him. He knew just what to say, he understood their feelings. He always raised a laugh at Hitler's expense and left his audience feeling they were a fine people bravely enduring hardship for the Cause—as indeed they were.

In Hull, knowing there was sufficient time, I left the train and wandered about looking at the town. Presently I heard roars and cheers, and there he was, sitting on the back of an open car, making the V-sign, hat in hand, on his way to the Town Hall. He was obviously pleased with the warm reception. It brought quite a lump to my throat; he deserved it, and lots more.

We went again to the north of England on various occasions, and I was lucky to be able to see most of the northern cities, including York and its great Minster. One of the reasons I always loved going on train trips was that the dining-car seemed to provide such wonderful meals. Even by that time in the war this ranked as a matter of importance. Food was becoming scarce, and in any case it was generally extremely dull and stodgy.

One day early in December the war took a great turn. Japan attacked. We were now all in the same boat, the three Great Allies. In the office the wheels were whirring. I had had the weekend off, so hurried earlier than usual to work on the Monday. Mrs. Hill was very busy with dictation, and quite soon there was a call for someone to go into the Cabinet Room. I went.

The Prime Minister was pacing up and down. He looked keen, enormously alive, on top of his job. After all, things had just taken a turn, so that now he could feel more than mere confidence in Britain's survival and eventual victory—it was now a sure prospect. He said, "Shorthand", and continued walking about, muttering "Letter to the King—letter to the King." But what was this I was writing down? "Sir: I have formed the conviction that it is my duty to visit Washington without delay …", asking for Royal approval of his sudden plan to cross the Atlantic immediately. This letter was followed by a directive to General Ismay, giving instructions as to who was to be included in the party and what arrangements made. I staggered out to my typewriter, eyes bulging, feeling this heavy secret could probably be read from my countenance. The others, realizing something big was on, were tactful enough not to inquire.

Within a few days the party had left, travelling in the new battleship *Duke of York,* sister ship of the *Prince of Wales.* Again, there was no question of female staff being taken along, but Peter Kinna and a young Air Force Sergeant, Geoffrey Green, were lent, as before, for the occasion.

So ended 1941.

8

For the first eight months of 1942 nothing seemed to go right. It was just one setback after another. First we had bad news from Cyrenaica—our forces were pushed back and Benghazi retaken by the Germans. Then the German warships *Scharnhorst, Gneisenau* and *Prinz Eugen* broke out of Brest and, speeding up the English Channel, evaded the attacks of our aircraft and shore batteries and regained home waters. In February Singapore fell to the Japanese. In June we lost Tobruk and were pushed back almost to Cairo. The U-boat warfare was taking a sickening toll, the Atlantic lifeline was stretching thin. The Russians were engaged in bitter fighting, and now at home uninformed clatter for a "Second Front Now", to take the weight off them, became irritatingly audible.

Throughout this period of stress and disappointment—to use his own words "a time to suffer and endure"—Mr. Churchill remained calm, firm, bulldog-jawed. As already mentioned, he was an easier person when times were hard; always at his most brilliant in a crisis, he seemed to draw on reserves of strength and will-power. He felt our losses very deeply, and threw himself anew into the task of hitting back. I think it was the lack of complete unanimity at home that troubled him as much as anything.

At the end of January, urged on by signs of restlessness among a small minority in the House of Commons, the Prime Minister made an enormously long statement on the war situation. A debate followed, which he was to wind up. On that occasion Mrs. Hill and I had one of our periodic near-misses. He only finished dictating his winding-up speech during the luncheon interval at the House, and thereafter the two of us sat at our machines in the Private Secretaries' room adjoining his office there, typing out the Speech Form as for dear life, without daring to look up from our desks. The Private Secretaries on duty, who would always rally round in a crisis, stood waiting for the pages, practically snatching them from the machines as we finished, to check, klop and tag them. When the Prime Minister finished speaking for the second time, a Vote of Confidence in the Government was taken, which he won by the substantial margin of 464 to 1.

I was always glad when it was necessary for one or both of us to go to the Prime Minister's room at the House. The place, as can well be understood, seemed heavily charged with the dignity of the years. One felt it almost a presumption to speak above a whisper. The chimes of Big Ben sounded so loud and near, and the Division Bell (calling for a vote in the Chamber), seemed to announce that the course of history was being moulded. Steeped in tradition and ancient custom, the place made one feel humble and ignorant, and the times we live in rough and rude.

The Prime Minister's room was panelled beautifully in linenfold, and contained a table and fifteen leather-covered chairs for meetings. I looked everywhere in the panelling for a secret door, but could find none.

Once I met Mr. Lloyd George in the corridor, his white hair and moustaches gleaming. In those days formal dress was worn. Later, when the Labour Government came in, I noticed they had installed a cafeteria downstairs, where Members and their secretaries together slid trays and ate pork pies. I thought it perfectly horrible!

To return to the year 1942, in March there was a Commando raid on the port of St. Nazaire, in the mouth of the Loire River. This was, of course, under the direction of the Chief of Combined Operations, Admiral Mountbatten, and during the weekend when the attack took place he was at Chequers with Mr. Churchill, awaiting news of the results as it came in. At first it seemed that all had not gone quite as planned. An old destroyer called the *Campbelltown* had been sunk in the harbour of St. Nazaire to prevent shipping moving in and out, but had not blown up as planned. Much damage had been done to the dock by the landing party. Thrilling and moving reports came in of the fighting, which amounted almost to a suicide job for the Commandos. Late in the evening Admiral Mountbatten came into the office, flashing his charming smile so that I nearly swooned under the desk with delight, and asked me to get through to Buckingham Palace. He wanted to give His Majesty the latest reports. Later we heard that the *Campbelltown* had after all blown up, luckily when a good number of Germans were aboard her. Here was a bright spot to cheer us on.

In June Mr. Churchill went again to Washington, this time by flying-boat. It was during this visit that he received the news of the fall of Tobruk. Deeply concerned, scarcely able to believe it—for he had said that we should hold Tobruk at all costs—he turned to his great friend for consolation. And not in vain. President Roosevelt's sympathy took a very practical form, for he immediately offered that a shipment of Sherman tanks destined for American forces in the Middle East and already *en route,* should be diverted instead to the re-equipment of our Armies there. Mr. Churchill was never able to forget this instantaneous act of kindness.

Indeed, the sympathy and understanding, the knowledge of a common aim, which existed between these two leaders was a great force sustaining them both.

Mr. Churchill flew back to Britain not many days later, and the special train was sent to Stranraer, on the Scottish west coast, to meet him. I was on duty on this occasion. It was thrilling to see the great shape of the flying-boat, red and green lights flashing, emerging from the heavy cloud not far overhead, with a vibrating roar that seemed to shake one's teeth loose. He landed at 4 a.m. and came at once to the train, anxious for the latest news. The returning party were somewhat astonished to find us looking a bit weary and complaining of the hour—they had not altered their watches since leaving America and had only finished dinner half an hour earlier. The Prime Minister did not yet feel it was bedtime, so we settled down at once to a spot of work.

But the loss of Tobruk seemed to have brought to a head the feelings of restlessness in the House of Commons before mentioned, and within a few days of the Prime Minister's return he had to face a motion of no confidence in the central direction of the war, put forward by Sir John Wardlaw-Milne, a Conservative Member of Parliament. This was a horrid time for all of us in the office. We felt awkward and unhappy, as I am sure Mr. Churchill did, and wondered how it was possible that anyone British could wish for a substantial change in the direction of the war at that time. I think the main feeling of Sir John Wardlaw-Milne and his followers was that Mr. Churchill should not be acting at once as Prime Minister and Minister of Defence, and they wished to see him pass on the latter position to someone else. We didn't support that view; we couldn't think of anyone who could reasonably take his place in either capacity.

There was a debate on the Motion of Censure, which the Prime Minister was to wind up—that is, he had the last word—and two of us sat up all night till 6 o'clock putting into Speech Form a tremendous statement he had prepared, which would take him at least an hour and a half to deliver. I hung around in the morning helping with the alterations, then took Mr. Churchill's gold watch, which had ceased to run, to a little man for mending—it was difficult to find someone to do repair jobs in those days. At 1.30 I returned to his room at the House, in case he wanted to dictate anything further. The debate was to end at 5 o'clock and he was to "get up" at 3.30. He was having his lunch late, and as I sat behind the typewriter in readiness I noticed that he was irritated because the peas wouldn't stay on his fork. I knew that despite his lifetime of experience and his enormous strength and self-control in bearing trials, he was still human enough to feel worked up inside. It must have been a great strain on his composure, having to drop all other work to state his own case to his fellow-Members, when so much hung on what he did with every minute of his time.

At last he went off to the Chamber, and I was left minding the office. I felt tired and discouraged. Blast it, why must life always be such a battle?

At 5 o'clock the Division Bell rang, which meant that Members would leave their seats and walk from the Chamber by the two doors, the Ayes going through one door and the Noes through the other, this being the method of voting. Time passed—which meant that many were going out by one door—good; twenty minutes passed, and I felt better. Then suddenly back they came to the office with the news that the Motion of Censure had been defeated by 475 to 25. Mr. Churchill, looking calm and matter-of-fact, came over and asked me what had happened to his gold watch. I explained its main spring was broken, but that the repairer had sent his own watch as a replacement and had asked if the Prime Minister would honour him by using it. He took it, and thanked me for staying up all night. I nearly wept, feeling worn out and at the same time relieved that all was well, and honoured to be spoken to just as he came from his triumph in the Chamber.

It was always obvious after one of his long statements to the House that Mr. Churchill had expended himself. He would put everything into his deliveries; perhaps that was why they always hit the mark.

Those difficult days seemed to make us even busier and in more of a hurry than usual. The weight upon the Prime Minister was tremendous, keeping the nation as well as Parliament balanced under the succession of setbacks and failures, and at the same time driving forward with his plans; for at that time many plans were being formulated. If we did occasionally hear a little backwash of grumbling that the P.M. kept Cabinet members up until complete agreement was reached in self-defence, that by 2 a.m. no one else had any resistance left, we discounted such stories as an expression of weakness.

I think sometimes it must have helped Mr. Churchill to start late on a particular job and feel that it had to be done within a short time. There seemed no other explanation of the last-minute rushes which we found so wearing to the nerves. There seemed so many statements at that time to the House of Commons, as well as broadcasts to the nation, each of which would mean several days of intensive preparation and a final last flurry to get the Speech or Broadcast Form done. We never failed to finish in time, but sometimes it took until next day to recover.

It must have been at about this time that our Principal Private Secretary, Mr. Martin, became engaged. One day I walked into his office and found him looking rather flustered, replacing the telephone receiver, the matter having just been settled. We all thought a great deal of him, and were glad for his sake, but we teased him about his telephone courtship. Actually, with all he had to do it was a wonder that he did get himself engaged and married.

As 1942 progressed, so the news improved. The famous Malta Convoy got through despite heavy losses and a nerve-shaking ordeal, and Malta, our vitally important naval base in the Mediterranean, was refuelled and supplied, for the moment anyway. To me this episode, which was code-named PEDESTAL, always seemed the turning-point of the war, the time when the news, after being "bad", always "bad" for so long, despite adverse circumstances turned to "encouraging". There were several raids on the French coast by Combined Operations—notably the costly Dieppe affair—which gave us a feeling of activity. We had knowledge of things that were to come later in the autumn. And, of course, there were the Americans.

At about this time Generals Eisenhower and Mark Clark arrived in England, in preparation for our combined plans for the assault on Western North Africa. They were in frequent consultation with the Prime Minister, and we saw them almost every weekend at Chequers. The British Chiefs of Staff and Ministers concerned would be asked there also, and heavy consultations took place.

I slipped up rather badly on the occasion when I first saw the American Generals. We were at No.10, and during the afternoon I went upstairs to Mrs. Hill's bedroom for a short sleep, having been up late the night before and it being again my night on duty. There was a bit of a whirl on in the office when I left, but Mrs. Hill was in charge and I did not wait until the Prime Minister himself went for his afternoon rest. I flopped on to Mrs. Hill's bed, and had fallen into a heavy sleep when the telephone bell rang. It was the Private Secretary on duty—"Come—*hurry*". Stopping only to put my feet into my shoes and smooth my hair with my hands, I ran. The Prime Minister was conferring with Generals Eisenhower and Clark—it was one of his first meetings with them—and wished to compose a telegram to the President in their presence. Mrs. Hill was busy elsewhere. I went in feeling, and I am sure looking, perfectly terrible, as if waked from the dead. The telegram, which was of major importance, was quickly typed and dispatched.

Afterwards I worried somewhat about this episode. The Americans were still more or less strangers to Mr. Churchill. I knew they would be used to a very high standard in secretaries. They could not yet know of our peculiar hours. We were not able to be very smartly dressed—neither time nor coupons allowed for that; but one and all we made it a rule always to appear neat and groomed, hair in order and properly made-up. However, I told myself, as I had many times before, that we were working to win the war—nothing else counted, really—and made the others laugh with descriptions of my dreadful *faux pas*.

I think Mr. Churchill found the American Generals charming: they were tactful, modest, direct and most businesslike. They carried on the warm friendship established by Messrs. Hopkins, Winant and Harriman, all of whom had been many times to Chequers. We of the staff were surprised by their easy friendliness and lack of formality.

General Marshall also appeared, and we thought his bulldog jaw made him the nearest approach to the P.M. we had yet seen. To give an idea of the business that would be done at Chequers at the weekend at this time, I quote the following guest list—Mrs. Hill or I would make out such a list for each weekend. On this occasion the idea was to acquaint General Marshall with various of the British leaders.

The Prime Minister Mrs. Churchill Mr. Harry Hopkins General Marshall Mr. Brown (Private Secretary) Commander Thompson	Arrive Friday evening to stay weekend.
Admiral Pound General Brooke Air Marshal Portal General Ismay	To dine and sleep Friday.
Lord Leathers Lord Cherwell	To lunch and dine Saturday.
Air Marshal Douglas	To dine Saturday.
General Nye Admiral Mountbatten Admiral Cunningham	To dine and sleep Saturday.
Mr. Oliver Lyttelton	To lunch and dine Sunday.
Air Marshal Harris General Eaker (U.S.A.)	To dine Sunday.

Mr. Harriman General Paget Mr. A. V. Alexander	To dine and sleep Sunday.

The planning of TORCH, the American and British descent on the North African coastline, was an operation with which we were constantly in touch, it being near home. It brought something new into our lives. At last we were going over to the offensive. After the ordeal of the bombing and the many losses and setbacks we had suffered, here we were planning something actual with our great friends, the Americans. For the Prime Minister, who earlier in the year had resisted the appeals for a "Second Front Now" and other suggestions for premature action, and no doubt had hated the necessity for doing so, it must have been a wonderful relief to have such a substantial offensive in prospect. Mr. Churchill kept President Roosevelt well in the picture with long telegrams, and so it seemed to be happening under our very noses. There was also in preparation the great British and Commonwealth attack in the Desert, at Alamein. We felt sure these ventures would succeed, and that our star was about to rise.

Dictation now took on a different form. We wrote of nothing but landing-craft, seaborne troops, escorting destroyers and anti-aircraft guns. One night on duty I was delighted to pick out a Winston touch. As he was writing something by hand on a document I heard him saying to himself, "Battalion—two t's and one l." Then he looked up and explained, "When I was small I always used to think of 'battle lions' to remind me of the spelling."

In August we knew that Mr. Churchill had a new plan—he was going to visit Moscow. From the first it was clear that there was not the vaguest hope of our being "in on this party"; Peter Kinna was booked to fly in the Prime Minister's aircraft and no females were required. The excitement was terrific, and when they all came back there were wonderful stories of banquets that went on until 4 a.m., of Russian officers being lifted from a recumbent position on the floor and carried off to bed, of toasts and more toasts, vodka, caviar, pink champagne—*ad infinitum*. How I longed to go to Moscow!

9

We now had two great offensive actions on hand. LIGHTFOOT, which was the code-name for the attack in Egypt, was to begin on the 23rd October, under the command of two new Generals in that quarter—General Alexander, the new Commander-in-Chief Middle East, and General Montgomery, in command of the Eighth Army. TORCH, the landings in Western North Africa, was due to start on the 8th November, under the general command of General Eisenhower.

For the last month or so before the time there was a more-than-usual air of tension in the office. One had to be particularly careful not to talk about dates! The North African landings were, I suppose, the more important strategically, especially as the Americans were in on this too; this was the climax to the three years of war past; this was the answer to the screams for a "Second Front Now": this would divert enemy forces from the Eastern front and so take some of the weight off Russia. All the same, I think the lesser action, later to be called the Battle of Alamein, had a place very near Mr. Churchill's heart. He was tired of the ups and downs of the desert warfare; he wanted to avenge Tobruk and see North Africa cleared of the enemy.

Luckily for me, it so happened that I was on duty the weekend just after LIGHTFOOT started. Everyone was in a wonderful humour, and much of the weekend was spent hanging about the office in great excitement, waiting for reports to come in on the telephone. Everything that was received over the Scrambler had to be typed out like the wind and rushed to the Prime Minister wherever he was, at meals, entertaining guests, walking in the garden, and so on. One afternoon a few days later the news of the great victory came through, and that evening when I went in for dictation the atmosphere was most jovial. I noted in my diary: "He and a few others were gathered in his study, full of jokes and laughter, he trying to dictate through it all, making me laugh too. Once he began to bark at me, then quickly stopped himself and said: 'No, no; quite all right—*quite* all right. Tonight you may rejoice. Tonight there is sugar on the cake.'"

And when TORCH started, two weeks later, it was again my weekend on duty, and we had a similar performance. The Prime Minister could hardly bear us to leave the telephone, and kept asking, "Any news?—well, ring up and ask again, that was twenty minutes ago." Something of particular interest would be shared with the Foreign Secretary. One would get him on the line, and Mr. Churchill would either report himself or order one to read over one's shorthand notes. The news seemed all good, and that for us was a considerable change. Mr. Churchill was in a wonderful humour, making us laugh in the office in the way he so easily could whenever he felt like it.

We were all tremendously relieved at the turn the war had taken, and though there was no relaxing, at least there was less anxiety. We felt more light-hearted than for many months. I recall one afternoon the Archbishop of Canterbury came to see the Prime Minister on Church affairs. He left his hat, a beautiful affair with little whiskers all over it, on a chair outside the room, and, feeling gay, I could not resist trying it on and doing a little dance. Even the Private Secretaries unbent, and our weekends on duty were far merrier than they had been. I remember Mr. Peck—he was always amusing—making me laugh very much by describing how one of my colleagues had got into hot water the night before. She had put "port" instead of "fort", and subsequently "fort" instead of "port". The Prime Minister, highly incensed, strode up and down, cigar well to the fore, at his most indistinct. "Good Heavens," he grumbled, "what's wrong with your hearing? Can't you tell the difference between a hort and a hort?"

Another evening at Chequers we were working late when a bat got into the Great Hall, where Mr. Churchill was walking about preparatory to dictating. Round and round it flew, occasionally making darts towards the fireplace. Mr. Churchill, irritated, came and sat in the office, but unfortunately the bat followed him there. I was frankly terrified, having never liked bats, and longed to run. Then Commander Thompson, unobserved, turned the table lamp upwards—it was one of the tilting variety—and the light on the ceiling drove the bat lower. The P.M., furious but intent on his subject, continued dictating, his face flushed and his jaw out, and I sat shrinking over the typewriter, occasionally ducking, while the others enjoyed the scene and grinned broadly in the background.

At just about that time I had, one day, a (to me) particularly interesting piece of dictation. The Prime Minister received from the Chief of Combined Operations a report on the possibility of using ice floes from the North as airfields. This idea, which had received the exciting code-name of HABBAKUK, was in preparation for our landings on the continent of Europe. Mr. Churchill took it up eagerly and strode up and down, voicing all sorts of possibilities. To me there was something very thrilling in the idea of an iceberg being harnessed to give service, even if it did sound a rather fantastic prospect. I was most disappointed when nothing more was heard of the HABBAKUKS. It was like the Prime Minister that he should seize so eagerly on an idea of that nature—perhaps it appealed to him too.

And then during the latter part of November, as luck would have it, Mrs. Hill became ill. She had been strained and unwell for some time, and now it was found that she had to have her appendix out. It was out of the question that the Prime Minister should be disturbed at that moment by having someone temporarily on his staff, and Peter Kinna was brought along to help me out. He remained on the Prime Minister's staff for the rest of the war, in a clerical capacity; he didn't really like shorthand and typing, and in the intervals between trips, when he did these things, he minded official documents and filing, arranged transport and so forth. This meant, however, that I was to be on duty almost every morning, taking over Mrs. Hill's times, often at night too, and almost every weekend. Peter Kinna would do night duty, but he could not do Speech Form, nor could the third on the personal staff, and that meant that all speeches and broadcasts were my final responsibility. And then, oddly enough, the third on our staff went down with a nervous breakdown and had to leave the office for good. Life was so overwhelmingly full that there seemed no time to settle down and think what to do—we just carried on as we were, hoping fervently that Mr. Churchill would not be put out by this depletion of his staff, waiting for Mrs. Hill to return, and trying to keep up with the work. At least the news was good, and that helped.

From that time, the end of November, until the Prime Minister left for the Casablanca Conference on the 12th January, was a hard spell for me. Everything seemed to happen that could happen. The gold pen, an indispensable part of our daily life, gave in, and I had to find someone to repair it, someone who could be trusted not to gain publicity from the job—which was a factor we had always to consider. Mr. Churchill's glasses ceased to give satisfaction: the regular oculist was away, and I had to find another, have his eyes tested for new glasses and fetch the latter when they were ready—in those days things were not delivered. On the 30th November there was The Birthday to attend to—piles and piles of telegrams and letters and presents to be acknowledged, in addition to the normal routine. I had to take responsibility for all his private affairs—letters, household accounts, constituents, gifts, engagements, literary affairs, Chartwell—all of which I had done formerly under Mrs. Hill's eye, so that it wasn't too difficult. I was even consulted on occasion by the Private Secretaries, which great honour made me giggle. I hardly had a day off in all that time. When Christmas came there was the usual list to be prepared of suggested names to whom gifts were to be sent (usually these were copies of Mr. Churchill's books), to whom telegrams were to be dispatched, and then these to be sent off.

I made plenty of mistakes, I was continuously tired, but I tried my very best. Anyone with any heart would have done so, knowing it would have caused disruption and discomfort if one had given in. Through all that time Mr. Churchill was kind and considerate—in fact, he was perfectly sweet to me, and I never had a hard word from him. I was immensely grateful for this. I suppose he saw how much I hated being ticked off. Though always an exacting employer, from that time on he was never really cross with me again—in fact, I give him full marks for kindness, generosity and loyalty to his staff. Mrs. Churchill, too, who would depend to a certain extent on my help at the weekends, could not have been kinder.

The P.M. made me smile one day. I was so bold as to point out a slight error in a direction he had given me, and he turned to me in surprise. "Quite right, quite right; take a good mark. Or rather, cancel the last bad one I gave you." I suppose he thought too many congratulations might produce too much self-confidence.

When he left for the Casablanca Conference I didn't even resent it that Peter Kinna and Geoffrey Green were to be taken and I was not. All I wanted was peace, perfect peace. Mrs. Hill was almost recovered; my vigil was over. When the evening came for him to leave, I noticed that the Private Secretaries who were not going with him were congregated around the door of the flat, waiting to bid him *bon voyage*. I did not quite like to join them, but I picked up Smokey, knowing the Prime Minister would notice his little cat, and stood some way off. Sure enough, when he emerged from his room, pink and beaming, ready to leave, he came and talked to Smokey, hugged him and told me to see he was not lonely. Then he shook hands and smiled, leaving me childishly pleased that Smokey and I had had more attention than the Private Secretaries.

Shortly after his return from this trip, which included a visit to Turkey following on the Conference, Mr. Churchill became ill. He must have been tired, for he seemed suddenly to be stricken with pneumonia almost before we knew he was unwell. For some days we wondered whether or not he would live. We were all utterly miserable; he was in his room at the Annexe, and most of the time we hung forlornly about the flat feeling quite lost. On the rare occasions when he dictated, and it could only be on a matter of major importance, his voice was so weak and his manner so gentle that we longed for the old stamp and bark, the quick word of scorn, the snort of impatience and the final twinkle of forgiveness. The flat was stiff with specialists, and two hospital nurses took up regular abode in the study. Eventually, to the relief of the whole nation, M. & B. won; and after a fortnight Mr. Churchill was well enough to travel to Chequers to convalesce.

And perhaps here is the right place to say a word about Mr. Churchill's personal doctor and great friend, Lord Moran. He was always in and out of the Annexe, constantly watching and checking up on his charge, and was always ready at the shortest notice to put aside whatever he was doing and accompany the Prime Minister on his travels by land, sea or air. He was a great favourite with us in the office.

On this occasion, on his instructions we remained at Chequers for ten days, and from the office there the affairs of Great Britain were conducted. I should think the household staff heaved many sighs of pleasure when we left.

One day while we were there we heard that the King proposed to visit Mr. Churchill. This was quite an unexpected honour. The Prime Minister was in the habit of lunching with His Majesty once a week, to report on the war and affairs at home. But now it was a few weeks since this had been possible, and King George had expressed the desire to see Mr. Churchill, who was still not well enough to travel to the Palace or to Windsor. The Coldstream Guards were alerted to produce a Guard of Honour, and thoroughly primed in the intricacies of a Royal Salute. The young officer who was to be Guard Commander was in a high state of nerves. When the great moment came and the long, black car, signalled by the police at the outer gate, drove into the courtyard, he fairly shrieked his order and a crashing salute was given. However, the car door opened and Lord Cherwell hurried into the house—it was the wrong car. When, a few minutes later, His Majesty arrived, all the stuffing seemed to have left the poor Guard.

It was during this period at Chequers that Mr. Churchill dictated his broadcast on post-war plans, his "Four Years Plan". One day he decided to drive to Dytchley Park for luncheon, a distance of about forty miles from Chequers. It happened that I was on duty, and he said that by the time we returned he would have dictated the bulk of the broadcast. And so it turned out. From the moment the car started till we reached our destination he raced along, his ideas tumbling over one another. He spoke of Reconstruction; of National Insurance; of Employment, the Export Trade, and Agriculture; he continued with Health and Education. But the journey home was even worse. He dealt with Rebuilding, Income Tax, National Finance, and our Wartime Scientific Discoveries. We had to make time, and the swinging of the car round corners disturbed my Pitman's best. When we arrived back I hurried to the typewriter, wailing to all and sundry that I was in for a real raspberry and couldn't someone please save me. They all clustered around—Mr. Martin, Commander Thompson, Lord Cherwell and other helpful people. What I had missed or could not read they made up for me: they told me what he had probably said and what they thought he ought to have said, and what they would have said had they been Prime Minister; and Mr. Churchill had later to admit that, while I had not recorded his dictation exactly, at least the words made sense. I escaped the raspberry.

And now I find I have not even mentioned the Prime Minister's Map Room, a place in which he loved to spend a few spare minutes and to which he often took visitors—if they were in the Secret circle. The Map Room had been set up by him in the Admiralty while he was First Lord, but at about that time it was moved to the Annexe close by the flat. It was run by a tall Irishman, Captain Richard Pim of the Royal Naval Volunteer Reserve, and his staff of R.N.V.R. officers who had been invalided out of active service. On the maps were marked the positions of our forces and, where known, of the enemy forces; shipping losses were shown, naval engagements, air attacks by both sides; the positions on the fighting fronts; U-boats, convoys, H.M. ships, and so forth. These were constantly revised, so that when the Prime Minister brought in an official visitor he could at once be shown the present position on any front so far as it was known. It really was most interesting. The Map Room was also a news centre. Each morning while we were in London a Map Room officer would present himself soon after Mr. Churchill waked, to give the latest news; and at all hours of the day or night somebody was on duty to report anything new or to investigate any inquiry we might wish to make. From the time of Casablanca onwards Mr. Churchill never travelled without a detachment from his Map Room, which always included Captain Pim, complete with maps, dividers and other trappings, so that wherever the Prime Minister was, even aboard ship, a Map Room could immediately be set up.

I must admit that sometimes we resented the Map Room boys a bit. To our way of thinking, they didn't work particularly hard; they oozed glamour and success; and they managed to be in on every darned thing that was going. But they were pleasant company and always had time for a friendly chat.

So the early months of 1943 passed. The news continued to be good, generally speaking. There were ups and downs in North Africa, naturally, but overall, our attacks prospered from both directions. In addition, the Battle of the Atlantic seemed to have turned in our favour.

With the end of hostilities in North Africa in sight, it became obvious that the Prime Minister and the President would have to meet again. After some inquiries to and fro, it was decided that Mr. Churchill should go again to Washington, taking with him various Cabinet Ministers, the Chiefs of Staff and their own staffs, and the Indian Commanders-in-Chief, Admiral Somerville, Field-Marshal Wavell and Air-Marshal Peirse, who came to England for that purpose. These dignitaries were to be transported in the *Queen Mary,* and their staffs would include a good number of young women. There was now no excuse for us to be left behind, but it seemed that Messrs. Kinna and Green were again on the sailing list. I *longed* to go, and as Mrs. Hill did not seem very keen, I screwed my courage to the sticking-point and asked, though by the time my request could be attended to it was only twenty-four hours before the time of departure. The reply was immediate—"If you wanted to go, why didn't you ask sooner?"—and so without further ado I rushed home, washed and ironed frantically, and presented myself at the Annexe in time for the train which was to bear the party northwards. I was ready to take off with delight, and was much envied by all the other Young Women in the office.

The signed portrait of Churchill which he gave to the author.

The Hawtrey Room at Chequers in which the Prime Minister often used to dictate.

10

We travelled overnight, Clyde-bound. I was in the seventh heaven. The last two years had been full of hard work and nerve strain, overtiredness, anxiety, and always one's best foot forward: underneath I was already feeling worn out. But here was something new, intensely thrilling; to have a place in the thrice-blessed crowd who went on Trips!—to eat American food!! Something to take one out of one's physical tiredness and give one a boost forward for the years of war still to come.

I was, of course, the only female in Mr. Churchill's personal party; Peter Kinna and I were to work together, Geoffrey Green's name having been taken off the list. Peter was decidedly on the short side, and I being 5 feet 8 inches, we made a good pair. We were to travel much together in the months to come, and to experience a very happy association. We grumbled together, sometimes giggled, frequently yawned and, I'm sorry to say, sometimes criticized the Private Secretaries, whose status was more elevated than our own.

Here is the beginning of the diary I wrote of this, the first of my Trips:

"Left the Annexe at midnight to join the train. Terrific security. I went to bed quite soon. The others in the sleeper (first-class sleeping coach with twelve compartments) were General Ismay, Lord Leathers, Lord Moran, Mr. Harriman, Lord Beaverbrook, General Wavell, Admiral Somerville, P.S. (meaning Private Secretary), Commander Thompson and Sawyers (besides me and the shower cubicle). Must admit I didn't sleep much. HE worked all morning and the time flew. In his tiny compartment the only place to sit was on the bed, squashed up trying not to land on his feet. Bad moment when I got cramp in one leg. However, all went off all right and we reached Gourock (on the Clyde) at 4 p.m. Went aboard a little tug where all the red tabs and gold braid in creation were congregated—just over 100 in the party—and were taken out to *Queen Mary*. She looked pretty huge in her dirty blue-grey camouflage, three funnels smoking, but not as big as I had imagined. Peter and I trotted aboard on Master's heels, were conducted to a lift, shot up several floors and then followed our guide down corridors and round corners till we came to our own abode.

"It is on Main Deck and might be considered a sort of Royal Suite. Mr. C. has a flat for himself and Sawyers, our Office opposite, and palatial rooms alongside in a row for Mr. Rowan, Commander Thompson, Peter and me. Of course, immediately we entered the doorway he wanted to dictate a letter to Mr. Andrews on his retirement as P.M. of Northern Ireland—and where were typewriter and paper? After considerable flapdoodle they arrived and all calmed down, letter was dispatched with extra P.S. who then left, and we sailed."

The crew of the little tug which took us from the dock to the *Queen Mary* (which would not normally dock at Gourock) had been astonished beyond words to see the parade of well-known faces, finally the Prime Minister's. This was, after all, the first mass crossing of the Atlantic by those at the head of affairs. After delivering us, the tug was taken farther up the Clyde and there moored, its crew imprisoned upon it, until it was heard we had reached the other side. No leakage was possible from that source.

Mr. Churchill did not dictate a great deal on the journey, as his days were chiefly occupied by conferences with the Chiefs of Staff: therefore there was a little time to get to know some of the people aboard. I joined up with some of the Cabinet Office girls, for company, and was introduced to many of those present. It was astonishing to me to eat breakfast or walk the deck with some of the most famous people in the land, for the time being on seemingly equal terms. Of our own Chiefs of Staff we saw nothing, but I was entranced by tall, good-looking, brown-eyed Air-Marshal Peirse, who seemed willing to talk about quite ordinary things, and bluff, merry Admiral Somerville, who teased us all and loved to make us laugh. One morning at breakfast I quite came out of my shell, and laughed teasingly at my neighbour, an Army officer in battledress; but I was horrified and silenced a little later to notice the crossed swords on his shoulder—a full General! However, he didn't seem to mind, and afterwards asked me to a party in Washington. Being the only girl in Mr. Churchill's party I was somewhat fussed over, especially as sometimes just when I had escaped for a little from the office a messenger would come urgently up and announce that the Prime Minister wished to see me … and I daresay those to whom I was talking thought to themselves, "Rather her than me." However, I can truthfully say that far from feeling pleased with myself, I was shy and uncertain, and quite glad to get away from the Generals and Admirals.

I was, however, glad and honoured to talk for a fleeting moment to General Wavell, the soldiers' hero. He looked just like his pictures, with his one sightless eye, and he seemed shy, a most unpretentious hero.

One event caused much mirth. The *Queen Mary* had just returned from transporting the Australian 9th Division somewhere or other, and thereafter had received a thorough preparation for her important cargo, part of the ship being restored to pre-war conditions. But alas, all the bugs had not been killed off; they had been moved backward, but as the days passed they flowed forth once more, and encroached farther and farther towards the central command, the P.M.'s own suite. Each day a new, higher stratum of officers would appear at meals red-faced and bitten, and had the journey taken longer I think the Chiefs of Staff and ourselves would have suffered. As it was, those at the core escaped the indignity.

The journey was made happy by the news of the war that was received *en route*. At the outset Admiral Pound was able to tell the Prime Minister he had just heard of the certain killing of five more U-boats. Then we heard of the fall of Tunis and Bizerta to the Allied Armies, and thereafter the war in North Africa was at an end. The Russians were making progress. And in the West our air offensive was growing, 2,000 tons of bombs in one night being the latest record.

Peter and I were not idle. All messages came in through us, and naturally the Prime Minister had to be kept completely informed. There were few early nights. Going westward meant that each night we had an extra hour of time, the clocks being put back at midnight. Mr. Churchill always made the most of this, playing bezique with Mr. Harriman till far into the night, with the excuse that he was sure they had forgotten to alter the clocks yet and "it can't be more than three o'clock, which means only two by the new time"—till poor Mr. Harriman looked quite haggard.

One day Mr. Churchill wrote a short note of congratulation to General Wavell aboard, which tickled my childish fancy. "Your combinations are an example of the military art." I wondered how military combinations differed in shape from the ordinary variety.

We were escorted all the way, the naval ships straining to keep up by sailing straight while we zigzagged. As we approached the American continent we were met by six American naval ships, which divided in half and steamed alongside us in Indian file.

We landed at Staten Island, just outside the New York harbour, were offloaded and put straight on to a train, which rushed us through to Washington. But before we arrived there we ate luncheon, our first American meal, and what a meal it was! We had all been waiting for this for some time, and when the steaks appeared they seemed not only to cover the whole plate but to touch the tablecloth on either side.

Arrived, Peter and I hastened to set up office in the White House. The Prime Minister had been allocated the same rooms as on his previous visits, on the first floor and to the left, past the famous President's Study. The whole floor, which was at slightly different levels, had been fitted with wooden ramps so that President Roosevelt could be wheeled about without difficulty.

Opposite our office was the bedroom of Mr. and Mrs. Harry Hopkins. Lanky, brown-eyed, sparse-haired Mr. Hopkins gave us a kindly welcome. He was the constant liaison officer between President and Prime Minister, and I think he knew and understood the President's mind better than anyone. He was always regarded by us as a great friend of Britain, and I wonder if his service to the Allied cause has ever been fully appreciated. His health was fragile, but his courage was boundless.

Of course, as soon as possible I put through a long-distance call to my mother in Vancouver, and soon we were conversing, much to her surprise.

The three weeks we spent in Washington were some of the busiest days I can remember. We seemed to pick up some of the American ideas of rush and bustle, and we fairly panted along from early morning until far into the night. There was a great deal to be done—two speeches, countless reports of meetings, messages to and from the War Cabinet, directives, Minutes, letters to Mrs. Churchill, as well as work for Mr. Rowan, the Private Secretary. Even at this time of year it seemed oppressively hot in Washington. There were huge portable rubber fans in every room at the White House, and these would sometimes make a positive junk-pile of our papers, but we were glad of them all the same. The heat, combined with the sudden change to rich food, made us feel a little under the weather at first, but we soon became acclimatized.

The White House staff obviously thought Peter and me quite mental to put up with our hours of work. Sometimes we finished only at 4.30 a.m. We kept reminding each other that we hadn't been brought along for a good time, and with the hustle in the office during the day we found the night the best time for getting a long job done. We took it in turns to have an hour or two off during the day, and only one of us remained on late duty. One evening, tottering off to bed at about 8.30 after a long day's work, I lost my way and accidentally joined an official reception for President Benes of Czechoslovakia, to whom all the notabilities of Washington were at that moment being presented. Mr. Mackenzie King was also staying at the White House: he remembered me from visits to Chequers, and sometimes came into the office to chat about Canada. Mr. Bernard Baruch, an old friend, called upon the Prime Minister; Lord Halifax, the British Ambassador, was frequently in attendance. I was too busy to "rubber-neck" and hardly noticed them.

There was the Home Guard broadcast. Mr. Churchill had promised to broadcast on the third anniversary of the formation of the Home Guard in Britain, and this was timed for 12.30 one day. But at 10.45 on that morning he was still sitting in bed, fiddling with his papers; the composing mood would not come. Suddenly he began to dictate, and we took it in turns, in shorthand. By 12.05 he had finished and was ready to rise and bath. Sawyers was called, and Peter and I went into full gallop to have his script ready. At 12.25 he emerged from his bedroom, looking pink and beaming and beautifully groomed, as he always did on these occasions, saying placidly in satisfied tones, "Well, I'm quite ready …"—and so, by the grace of God, was his broadcast. Panting, we handed it to him. He had only to cross to another room where microphones were set up, and five minutes later he was on the air.

A few days later the Prime Minister was to address the Congress of the United States. It was to be an important speech, a review of the whole war scene, and a night or so beforehand he got through most of the dictation. He had been dining and conferring with the President, but about midnight he came to his own quarters, saying that a busy night was in prospect. Mr. Rowan, who looked dead tired, was sent off to bed. I settled myself in Mr. Churchill's room with book and several pencils, in an armchair with high back and ear-flaps, and soon, as was his custom, he began pacing about the room. Inspiration came, and flowed on and on and on. Back and forth he walked, his hands gesturing, his voice rising and falling. About 2 o'clock a sleepy note came into his voice, and I knew he wouldn't last much longer. Presently while behind my chair he took off his dinner-jacket, then continued pacing the room. The next time he went out of sight he took off his waistcoat. I wondered in considerable amusement what would happen next. There was a longer pause than usual behind my chair, and a rustling sound as something flew through the air on to the bed. When next he appeared, he was wearing his famous green and gold dressing-gown with the red dragons, the cords trailing behind as usual.

At 2.30 he finished, and at 4.30 I finished typing it out. As I tottered off to bed, one of the American officers on duty near the front door said: "Gee, are you crazy? All the American girls went home just twelve hours ago."

It was a great thrill, during the hour or so which one managed to take off in daytime, to wander round the shops, so different from the bare-picked, utility-stocked shops of Britain, buying little reminders of better times for those at home. Always fond of food, I found great delight, too, in sitting on a stool in a

Washington drugstore and ordering a sickly ice-cream, or a peanut-butter-and-cream-cheese sandwich. One of such expeditions was cut short by a sudden heavy downpour of rain, and I was forced to engage a taxicab to take me back to the White House. In those days of wartime, taxis were shared, and there were already three or four people sitting in the one I encountered. When I asked to be taken to the White House, the negro driver looked at me with respect. "Lady," he said, in a deep Southern drawl, "Ah've bin drivin' dis cab twenny ye'rs, and dis only de secon' time Ah've bin to de White House." The other occupants were considerably astonished when, the rain increasing in force, the cab was allowed to pass the gates and drive me to the very front door, on production of my White House pass.

One weekend of our time in Washington was spent at the British Embassy there. We packed up the office and transplanted, for a few days with Lord and Lady Halifax. The Embassy seemed to me like a little island of Britain in the midst of America, with Kings and Queens looking at one from nearly every wall. Mr. Churchill's bedroom was on the second floor, and as there was neither a bell to the butler's pantry nor a telephone to the office, most of my time was spent in sitting by his bedside and running every now and then for Sawyers or Mr. Rowan. There was a telephone of sorts in the room, however, and our first morning there the operator did not seem to know who had been placed in which room. During the morning session with the Box, the telephone rang several times in error. Each time I hastened to it, and tried to explain in hushed and hurried tones that this was the wrong extension and would the switchboard *please* not put through further calls. After two or three of these explanations, Mr. Churchill looked up rather pathetically. "Oh," he said, "next time, do tell them to SHUT UP."

As our visit drew to an end, activity in the office increased. It was decided that the Prime Minister and his personal party, with the exception of myself, should fly straight to North Africa, there to consult with Generals de Gaule and Giraud; I was to return with the main party in the *Queen Mary.*

The night before they left, Peter went off early and I was on duty alone. Presently, after dinner, Mr. Hopkins came walking into the office to inquire if I would like to meet the President. I jumped up in a terrific fluster, gasping that my nose was shining and my hands grubby—but he just smiled and said, "Oh, come along," so I went. Mr. Churchill and Mr. Roosevelt were dining alone in the latter's study, and as I entered with Mr. Hopkins they both looked up and beamed. The President said, "I think it's about time I met you," holding out his hand to shake mine, with that well-known toss of his head and the famous smile.

He spoke kindly to me for a few minutes, then I felt it was time to go and backed hastily out, with a grateful look at the Prime Minister, thinking this could not really be me at all. What I remember best about the President is his charming, cultured voice and his kind eyes.

It is not for me to make a summing-up of the figures of history; but I felt at the time that, while there were two persons of great stature in that room, one of them, though the less tolerant and the more positive, was the greater personality.

Later on Mr. Hopkins brought in a Press release which the Big Two wanted typed out again and again, as different drafts were tried. One version, a short note written in the President's handwriting, I was allowed to keep as a souvenir. At about one o'clock General Ismay appeared with a hefty document just drawn up by the Staffs, embodying the Conference decisions and results, known as the Conclusions. This was shown to the Prime Minister and the President, who hacked it about a good deal, and then I retyped it. There was not much sleep that night.

Next morning they flew off, and later that same day I set out for Montreal, on Mr. Churchill's instructions. It was some days before the *Queen Mary* was due to sail, and he arranged for me to spend the time at my brother's home. It was wonderful.

Finally, the balance of the party sailed from New York, in company with 16,000 American troops. It was rather different from the outward voyage, as fourteen young women shared one cabin, but we had plenty of fun and laughed at the wolf-whistles and cat-calls which our appearance on deck evoked.

As soon as we were home I noticed how much better I was feeling. It was the change, and the fun, and the good feeding-up. I wrote to my mother, "I feel a new zest towards Victory", and plunged forthwith into work.

11

I used to feel, in those days before I became more used to travelling around with Mr. Churchill, that I was in very truth the luckiest girl in the world. Walking in St. James's Park during the morning after a night on late duty I used to ponder this fact with much amazement. I had accompanied the Prime Minister on a trip overseas, the first of his female staff to do so. It seemed that President Roosevelt stayed at home more than we did. I doubted whether Marshal Stalin ever dashed across oceans in large ships. I—Elizabeth Layton from British Columbia—I was the luckiest girl in all the world! That was indeed something to marvel at. I never really came to take this for granted, though as time went on naturally it ceased to cause me such extreme wonder.

On the 30th June that year Mr. Churchill received the Freedom of the City of London. This took place in the ancient and historic Guildhall, badly battered though it had been in the fire blitz, and was followed by a luncheon at the Mansion House. There was great competition to obtain invitations to the ceremony; the Cabinet Ministers and their wives were, of course, invited, and all persons of particular distinction living in or near London who could be fitted into the not very spacious hall. Mrs. Hill and Ham, the two seniors among the personal staff, were given tickets of admission as being so closely interested in the matter, and the seniors among the Private Secretaries were also included. I longed to go, but there seemed not a hope. Mr. Churchill prepared a speech of moderate length and great eloquence, and the night before I had the task of putting it into Speech Form.

On the morning of the day in question we were informed that the Hon. Mrs. Keppel, a relation of Mrs. Churchill's, would not be able to attend, and her seat would therefore be vacant. Mrs. Hill asked Mrs. Churchill, then took me aside. "Keep it dark," she said, "you can go." I nearly fell on her neck.

There was an enormous crowd filling the City and making it difficult to move about, but at length I reached the Guildhall and found my place. I could see Mrs. Hill and the others sitting some way behind me, but Mrs. Keppel's seat was in the front row on the aisle up which the distinguished guests were to walk. Looking around one could see that most of the old monuments about the walls had been destroyed in the fire, and the beautiful roof was entirely gone, a temporary wooden affair keeping the place weatherproof. The walls were still blackened and shaggy from the flames.

At the front was the platform where stood the Lord Mayor, weighed down with gold chains, receiving those assigned to the platform seats, who were announced by the Herald as they entered. City Aldermen and others were clad in the colourful robes of their time-honoured offices. Well-known figures could be seen on all sides. My own neighbours turned out to be Sir Charles Howard, the Sergeant-at-Arms of the House of Commons, and an Air-Vice-Marshal, at that time Gentleman Usher of the Black Rod in the House of Lords, whose name I forget. They were quite chatty, but when they discovered I was not Mrs. Keppel as my card indicated they seemed a little shocked—when asked, I told them, "Well, I type."

At last the guest of honour arrived. The Herald announced "The Right Honourable the Prime Minister and Mrs. Churchill"; they were received by the Lord Mayor and seated on the platform. The City Chamberlain read an account of the Prime Minister's achievements, the Freedom ceremony was performed, and then Mr. Churchill rose to give his Address, which lasted about three-quarters of an hour.

This was the first time I had actually seen him make one of his deliveries, apart from the usual preview while he was dictating. As he took from his pocket the notes I had so recently typed, I wondered anxiously if the pages were in the right order.

It would be difficult to overstate the interest to be derived from seeing as well as hearing Winston Churchill speak, and I am sure there was not one in all that distinguished gathering who did not feel the rare privilege it was to be present. He was, of course, looking most spick-and-span in morning-coat and striped trousers, and as he reached the small reading-desk from which he was to speak, he took out his glasses and put them on, a familiar act. From the moment he started on the formalities "My Lord Mayor …", etc., one realized how completely he was master of the situation, how un-anxious he felt. He knew he had a treat in store for the audience, he knew they knew it. They were not disappointed.

Mr. Churchill spoke very much as he always did on the radio—slowly but not too slowly, clearly and emphatically, so that one wondered why one had found it difficult to understand him when one first knew him. He made use of every pause, his sense of timing was perfect—he might not have been reading from his notes but speaking his thoughts as they came to him. His hands gestured in the well-known fashion; sometimes he would hold the front of his black coat, fingers tucked in, sometimes his hands would be clasped in front of him, sometimes a forefinger would be uplifted. He held his audience (me included) spellbound, and I am convinced there was no one present who did not feel a prickling thrill in his veins when Mr. Churchill said, in that growly way one knew so well, "It is very probable there will be heavy fighting in the Mediterranean and elsewhere before the leaves of autumn fall."

Afterwards various little ceremonies took place, then the Lord Mayor escorted Mrs. Churchill down the aisle, followed by the Prime Minister with the Lady Mayoress. As he passed me Mr. Churchill looked surprised and said "Oh—hullo", much to the astonishment of my neighbours, who seemed quite impressed.

The next event of prime importance was our invasion of Sicily, operation HUSKY. One Friday on our way to Chequers the Prime Minister called at the Admiralty, where in the War Room a huge map had been set up showing the ships of the attacking forces, British and American. He stayed a long time studying this, and speaking in great seriousness to the Duty Officer. Everyone was tense; the weather was not good, too much wind, and it seemed possible that even now, with the ships steaming on their way, the landings would have to be postponed. However, after a rather sleepless night at Chequers we learnt in the morning that everything had taken place according to plan, with results now well known.

Not long after this I had some welcome news, for which I had been longing. I was to be included in the Prime Minister's staff to attend the First Quebec Conference, which was to take place early in August. It seemed almost too good to be true—Canada! Peter and Geoffrey Green were also to go, and in addition my friend Ham, since Mrs. Churchill and Mary, the latter in her Army uniform, would accompany the Prime Minister.

We sailed once more from Gourock in the *Queen Mary,* Ham and I sharing a cabin. This time there was more work and less social life. The Chiefs of Staff were aboard with their staffs, and the ship was just a miniature Whitehall. We landed at Halifax—I believe the *Queen Mary* had never docked there before—and travelled by special train to Quebec, where at Wolfe's Cove Mr. Mackenzie King was waiting to welcome the party. *En route* we passed through some lovely country and many small towns, where the news of the Prime Minister's arrival seemed to have spread in advance, for crowds were awaiting him at every station and he made several appearances on the platform at the back of the train. Sitting beside him in the rear saloon, and seeing myself also somewhat the object of notice, I had the most absurd longing to jump up and shout, "Hi, I'm not English, I'm Canadian like you."

The main party was quartered in the Château Frontenac, which had been completely commandeered for Conference personnel—British, American and Canadian. The Prime Minister and his personal party were housed in the summer residence of the Governor-General, called the Citadel, a picturesque building on top of the hill overlooking Quebec, surrounded by stone ramparts over which could be seen the St. Lawrence hundreds of feet below. The walls were guarded day and night by Mounties in their scarlet coats.

Within a few days Mr. Roosevelt arrived, and now on the green square of grass next to the main building three flags were flown—the Union Jack, the Stars and Stripes, and the Canadian flag. We were rather amused to see the President's car—an open one—arriving smothered in Secret Service men, even when, sitting in it, he inspected a detachment of Mounties in the Citadel courtyard. They hung on the back and on the bonnet and from the running-boards. Mr. Churchill travelled with only his two Scotland Yard detectives, who would usually be on duty one at a time.

And now the whole of the Citadel was no longer free to us, the upper floor being occupied by the President and guarded by gorilla-like figures from the top of the stairs onward. This caused us many smiles. We were not used to worrying about our security from this angle. Once or twice, sent up there by the Prime Minister, I forced my way past the indignant guard to deliver a paper to the President's office, inviting them to shoot me in the back if they wished.

During this Conference we worked hard. A vast number of papers were turned out and, of course, close touch was maintained with the British Cabinet.

One day Mr. Eden arrived by flying-boat. Mr. Martin, our Principal Private Secretary, was at that moment connected by telephone to Mr. Attlee in London, and was forced to hang up owing to the roar of the aircraft as it circled the Citadel before landing in the St. Lawrence.

It was at this time that I first heard of the interesting possibility known by the code-name of TUBE ALLOYS, the Atom Bomb. While at Quebec I had a long paper to copy on the subject, which I was first warned was of exceptional secrecy and importance. I remembered my brother, long ago in our youth in British Columbia, talking about the eventual splitting of the atom, and suddenly the penny dropped—this was what they were doing. I felt ready to burst with this staggering information. For a long time after that, now that I was in on this secret, I was the one in the office to copy the TUBE ALLOYS papers. It very soon became just another facet of everyday life.

At the end of the Conference the Prime Minister made a world broadcast, speaking from the Citadel, and that same night we left by train—and oh, what a super-luxury train it was—for Washington, for the second part of the journey. And here I must include an incident which was typical of Winston Churchill. As we travelled south next day, I sitting by him waiting for dictation, he began asking about my mother, who had flown from Vancouver to see me during the Conference. Then he told me he wished to make her a present of half her fare across the continent, knowing what an effort she had made. I was touched, indeed, at his kindness. The fact that while pressed upon by matters of international importance he still never forgot those who worked for him, inspired feelings of real devotion in his staff which will be readily understood.

It was pleasant and familiar to enter the White House once more, and soon we were engulfed in a first-class flap. The office we normally occupied was not big enough to accommodate the two Private Secretaries, Peter, Geoffrey and me, and so we three were moved across the passage into a sitting-room, I think it was the Monroe Room, which in a very short time changed its appearance into that of a paper junk-shop. Everywhere were klops, tags, pins, clips, piles of carbon copies, papers to be sorted into the files, files to be sorted into the secret boxes, bags to be dispatched to London by carrier, and so on. For the first day or so I was too busy to find myself a proper desk, but set up my typewriter (our own noiseless machines travelled with us) on the rear portion of a grand piano, in front of which I sat on the back of an armchair. We seemed to take it in turns to whirl over to the other office, into Mr. Churchill's room and back to ours, and a good deal of typescript was produced. At this time the secret plans for that amazing invention, the Floating Harbour, the famous MULBERRY, were under discussion, and our office became also a waiting-room for all the scientific experts you ever heard of, a good number of whom seemed anxious to enlist our services the moment any of us looked like letting up.

One morning we had an anxious time. During this period Italy was being invaded by our combined forces, and just then Marshal Badoglio had agreed to sign terms of unconditional surrender to the Allies; this was to take place on the 3rd September. But when I reached the office for early duty that morning, there was the telephone ringing and ringing. No Private Secretaries yet about. It was Sir John Dill, Head of the British Joint Staff Mission in Washington—angry—why was nobody at hand?—why had the Prime Minister not been awakened? I was puzzled. Soon he rang off. I felt irritated—wasn't one Big Chief enough around the place? Then arrived a telegram by special messenger, marked with every sign of urgency and secrecy. I hastily opened and read it, realized its import and, feeling extremely bold, awoke the Prime Minister to show it to him. Some hitch had taken place—the agreement with Italy would not be signed.

Mr. Churchill looked very grave indeed and, as sometimes happened early in the morning, shouted at me impatiently for this and that paper, which I rushed about trying to find. Soon the President was wheeled into the bedroom for a conference, and then Sir John Dill arrived. But later in the day a further telegram was received from General Eisenhower—the difficulties had been solved and the agreement was to be signed. Collapse of staff, in relief.

After some days the Prime Minister, Mr. Martin, Peter and I left Washington by overnight train for Harvard, where Mr. Churchill was to receive an honorary Doctorate of Laws. Peter and I worked until 4.30, getting his speech ready, in our special train. The next day—or rather the same day—we had the honour and privilege of being present at the ceremony.

Perhaps the graduation "bonnet" which had been supplied to Mr. Churchill did not suit him as well as his more standard headgear. Nevertheless, one knew everyone in that hall was conscious of the presence of a very great man. I had the same sense of anxiety that his speech notes might be incorrectly prepared. But I need not have worried; that eloquent orator, that accomplished speaker was never more in his element, and held his audience rapt. It was a deeply impressive occasion.

We returned to the train, and in the late afternoon set off again for Washington. There was no work that night, and so Peter and I sat by the windows as the evening drew on, making V-signs to all we passed, much to our own amusement.

After a further period in Washington, we set out once more in our favourite train, on the homeward journey. This was broken at Poughkeepsie, for we spent a day at Hyde Park, with the Roosevelts.

It was to me an honour to enter the pleasant and comfortable home of the Roosevelt family. Peter and I were given the old nursery for our office, and I was delighted on looking around the shelves there to find a book which had been a favourite of my childhood, *The Little Duke*; this I paged through rather guiltily, the main party having gone out for a picnic lunch. Peter and I visited the Roosevelt Museum, which was housed near by, and were touched to note the care with which were preserved, alongside the treasures of the Roosevelt family, those little gifts which had been sent to the President by simple, loving people all over the country.

When the party returned, Mr. Churchill called me for dictation. He sat on the terrace in front of the house, in the warm afternoon sun, while the shadows slowly lengthened. There was a bluish haze over the firs and pines which grew on the hills sloping up from the Hudson River below. It was very beautiful and peaceful, and not at all like bomb-scarred London. Later, as we left to drive back to our train, a great yellow moon was rising behind the now black-silhouetted pine trees.

That night, *en route* for Halifax, Mr. Churchill had a terrific volume of dictation, mostly reports of his discussions with the President. I, on duty, sat writing until 2.30, when my eyes were nearly dropping out and I could no longer suppress my yawns. Finally, after a particularly obvious one, Mr. Churchill said impatiently, "Well, you'd better go to bed if you're tired, and type it out in the morning." My appearance must indeed have been rock-bottom, to have produced this rare indulgence.

We sailed from Halifax, but this time aboard the battle-cruiser *Renown,* sister ship of the lost *Repulse,* the main party from the Quebec Conference having already returned in the *Queen Mary.* As we pulled away from the dock, the band of the R.C.M.P., the Mounties, which was assembled there, struck up. They played "Rule Britannia", and **"O Canada"**, and "Will Ye No Come Back Again". I stood on deck, gazing at the receding shores of my dear land of Canada, shedding not a few tears. However, that feeling soon passed, especially as there was an enormous Review of the War to the House of Commons in preparation which gave one no time for feelings of nostalgia.

It was exciting to travel on a naval ship, in particular for Ham and me and about twelve Wren Cypher Officers from the Conference, as we were much spoiled by the officers, and when not working could always find some interesting company. Mr. and Mrs. Churchill were housed in the Admiral's quarters, high above the foredeck, and it did seem odd to sit beside the Prime Minister in the Admiral's Sea Cabin, while he worked away at his Box. The roll of the ship made it impossible to sit still, and his matches and pens were continually sliding about. He decided he would prefer to light his cigar with a candle, and it was my job to light this every half-hour or so and then take it into the adjoining bathroom to blow it out, so that the waxy smell did not reach him. I thought, like Alice, "Curiouser and curiouser."

On the first and second days at sea we were given demonstrations of shooting. We stood on a small deck just below the bridge, while the eight-inch guns and then the really big ones fired at a target towed by one of our escorting cruisers. There were some odd-looking, black, many-headed guns called Chicago Pianos. The noise was deafening; personally I was so glad when they stopped.

Another day I was walking the quarter-deck with a few of the officers, thinking His Lordship was still resting, when suddenly a Marine orderly appeared—"The Prime Minister would like to see you at once." My hair was standing on end in the stiffish breeze, but wasting no time in straightening it I hurried the considerable distance to the Admiral's Sea Cabin, snatching book and pencils from the office in passing, knowing it would be more Speech, and presented myself somewhat breathless, pink and tousled. Presently Mr. Churchill looked up gravely from his papers, and said with the utmost courtesy, "I do hope I didn't disturb you at your tea." I thought to myself, "Hope he doesn't take another look."

After eight days at sea we reached Plymouth, and so home to London. Before leaving the ship we all sang the sailors' hymn, "Eternal Father", on the quarter-deck, which remained in my ears for many months. We were glad to see our colleagues once more, but there was little time for chat, with the Statement to the House in only three days' time.

A week or so later it was announced that the second of the Private Secretaries who had accompanied us to Quebec, Mr. Rowan, was engaged to marry the prettiest of the Cypher Officers. It had been a whirlwind courtship, beginning at Quebec; they seemed a very well-matched pair. Here was Romance coming as the result of Duty. All the unattached in the office sat up and began to wonder when the next trip would be, and what their chances were of taking part in it.

12

After this interlude life went on as usual for a few weeks. We were visited at Chequers again by General Smuts, for whom Mr. Churchill always had a warm welcome—I always admired his voice, and thought the clipped South African accent attractive—and by General Carton de Wiart, V.C., recently released from prison camp in Italy, whose one sightless eye and missing arm gave him a romantic air. Then Admiral Sir Dudley Pound—that gallant old sea-dog, First Sea Lord until recently when ill health had forced him to resign—died and was given a State funeral. The Prime Minister insisted on marching behind the coffin down Whitehall to the Abbey, rather against medical advice, and we watched him, a dogged figure moving somewhat stiffly to the notes of Chopin's Funeral March, that bulldog look on his face which betokened the emotion he was feeling at the death of his old friend and colleague. Indeed, watching the procession pass, one felt like weeping too.

By way of contrast, I feel I want here to include the following extract from a letter I wrote at that time to my mother.

"Here we are back in the office, in much more drab surroundings than when I last wrote to you aboard *Renown*. Here in front of me is a most amusing cartoon by Low, and I'll just describe it to you. It is called 'Imitation the Sincerest Flattery', and at the top is written, 'It may be only Low's imagination, but many of the latest orations on the Nazi Home Front have a familiar ring.' Hitler and Goering are standing in front of a microphone; they are both wearing light-blue zipper siren suits and Winston hats (large and black), with huge cigars in mouths and large tummies. Hitler is waving clenched fists above his head and is broadcasting, 'Ve vill fight in der strassen … ve vill fight in der hills … in der fields … up der chimneys … under der tables. Dis is our finest hour, etc., etc.' There is a picture on the wall of Winston looking extremely Winston, in just the same garb, and under it is Written 'Der Criminaldipsomaniac Plutobolshevikjew Churchill—Ach—Ve Shpit', which I presume is the Teutonic version of That Bad Man."

We all knew that plans were afoot for the Cairo Conference and the first Big Three meeting at Teheran, and one evening as I sat waiting for dictation Mr. Churchill asked, out of the blue, "Do you want to come with me again?" *Did I?* ...

Early in November we embarked again in *Renown* at Plymouth and proceeded via Gibraltar and Malta to Alexandria. If it had been thrilling to sail westward, it was doubly so to be going east, to the unknown. The sky was blue and the sun was hot; the buildings of Alexandria, when we got there, were white and queer-shaped, the desert flat and never-ending. Never before had we seen such odd little donkey-carts, or such dirty, unkempt people as the Arabs who drove them.

I was rather sad to leave the ship, as for once I had found a Boy Friend. He was a Lieutenant with a beard, tall and rather artistic, named Michael. But he promised to write. I thought he was wonderful.

The Conference of the Staffs, preliminary to Teheran, was to take place at Mena House outside Cairo, and here the main body of the party were deposited. The Prime Minister and his personal party, which consisted of his daughter Sarah in W.A.A.F. uniform, two Private Secretaries (Messrs. Martin and Brown), Commander Thompson, Peter, Geoffrey and myself, Sawyers and two detectives, were accommodated in the villa of Mr. Richard Casey, then Minister Resident in the Middle East. It was about a mile from Mena House, and bore the romantic name of Beit el Azrak, which I discovered merely meant Blue House. It was a delightful villa, blue and white tiled, with crimson bougainvillea much in evidence. Within was a square courtyard around which the house was built; a small fountain played in the centre.

The place had been carefully fitted out to suit the Prime Minister. Everywhere were bells, buzzers, telephone extensions, mosquito nets, fly swats and the like. My first job was to make sure that all arrangements were in order—that HE could from his bedroom ring for Sawyers, buzz for a Secretary or speak by telephone to whom he chose, that his bed was securely netted against mosquitoes and his bedside table laid out with the correct selection of klop, tags, pencils, "Action This Day"s, and all the necessaries.

Soon we were comfortably settled in. We made our office into a fairly permanent sort of place, knowing our stay there was to be of at least three weeks. The Map Room was next door. Shortly after our arrival, President Roosevelt also arrived, with his large and efficient staff of Secret Service men, and was established in an equally comfortable villa about a mile past Mena on the Cairo road. A third leader made his appearance, Generalissimo Chiang Kai-Shek, and he and Madame occupied a third villa at no great distance from our own.

Peter, Geoffrey and I became at once engulfed in the usual atmosphere of haste. Papers had to be prepared for the consumption of the President, drafts for joint signature by the three leaders, preparations for Teheran, telegrams home to the Deputy Prime Minister and War Cabinet, and many other matters. Admiral Lord Louis Mountbatten arrived from Kandy, General Carton de Wiart from China, and these, as well as Lord Killearn, British Ambassador to Egypt, were constant visitors. Frequently they would drift into the office to see what action was in progress, or to the Map Room, where there was plenty to look at.

One never-to-be-forgotten evening the Chiang Kai-Sheks dined with Mr. Churchill and Sarah. The dining-room was just across the courtyard from the office, so that we had a good view of them as they sat at dinner and later when they inspected the Map Room. The Generalissimo looked old and very frail. He wore a black robe belted with a cord, and his thin, delicately-featured face had a transparent look as if he belonged to another world. His dignity and stately bearing were impressive. Madame was also dressed in black, but with a touch of white and a white flower in her hair. She looked a model of elegance and grooming, small, neat and vivacious, a brilliant conversationalist speaking fluent English with an American accent.

Mr. Churchill loved to sit in the sun next to the little fountain in the courtyard as he worked at his Box or dictated directives. Sometimes he would instruct one of the Royal Marine orderlies to stand by its tap. "It's too high," he would say, "turn it down." Then "Now a little up; no, a bit lower; just a bit higher …" and so on, until his full attention was claimed by his work. One afternoon in the warm sunshine he dictated a Press communiqué about Lord Louis Mountbatten, who had just been made Supreme Commander, South-East Asia Command. I well remember the wilting smile I received from the gallant Admiral, who was pacing about the courtyard, as he asked me to do an extra carbon copy for him!

A young army captain had been assigned to us as a sort of aide-de-camp in charge of arrangements. This was my first experience of these delicate young men, some even with peroxided hair, who seemed rather numerous in those parts as Personal Assistants to Generals, and so forth. This one certainly had matters well in hand; he was most efficient, polished and intelligent, and from the first surprisingly at home among our party. I fear we had a few smiles at his expense. He carried a beautiful switch with which he kept the flies at bay, and sometimes as he walked through the villa he would clap his hands for service from the Arabs. "Oh, Martin," he would say to our Principal Private Secretary, "So-and-so telephoned while you were out, so I just told him so-and-so"—which at first produced an explosive atmosphere and later broad grins. One day as I walked through the grounds with him, we came on some grubby little native boys lying in the grass. "Up, up," he said, flicking them to their feet with his fly switch. And in return for the doubtful raising of their hands to their foreheads, he gave them the most correct salute required by a visiting General. The Middle East was an interesting place all right.

The time came for the Teheran party to fly off. I remained at the Beit el Azrak, and therefore have nothing to tell of the first Big Three meeting. I did not resent this in the least. I was intensely happy. There were the Pyramids to visit, and the Sphinx, sandbagged to her chin. I loved to watch the camels and their ragged owners, seeming to have come straight from Bible days. Night fell so quickly in Egypt; the stars seemed so big and bright, and every night the cold, round moon shone down. Some of the Map Room boys were also left behind, and took me dancing. Thereafter I had a wonderful time and was snowed under with invitations. This was the life!

When they arrived back, all thoughts were turned on Turkish affairs, as the Prime Minister and President Roosevelt were to meet President Inonu here at Mena. Much urgent work was at hand. One morning the P.M. delivered himself of a most enormous paper on Turkey. I was doing my best to produce this in type, for nowadays he often liked one to use shorthand, and Peter was standing by to check, klop and tag, the matter being urgent. Several gentlemen of ambassadorial status, one of them Sir Hughe Knatchbull-Hugessen, our emissary to Turkey, came wandering into the small office, all anxious to know "what the P.M. had said". Vainly did we hint that if we were not left alone, no one ever would know. Finally Peter hustled them politely out of the door, promising each he should be the first to receive a carbon copy. Afterwards we looked at one another grinning, and remarked that we were getting hardened indeed if we could order Ambassadors about.

A few days later President Roosevelt and President Inonu dined with the Prime Minister, together with various of their advisers. Among them was Monsieur Menemencioglu, and watching them across the courtyard I could not help thinking of the occasion when, taking dictation on the typewriter in faraway No.10, I had first heard his name. I had stopped and goggled, and Mr. Churchill had said impatiently, "Come on now, you know that one", and when I had anxiously handed over the Minute for initialling he had been surprised into congratulations because by some strange chance I had spelled it right.

The Conference ended on an optimistic note. Decisions had been taken. Something had been achieved, some progress made. A moderate satisfaction seemed to spread itself. After a few days of winding up, the Staffs prepared to leave, but for Mr. Churchill and his own party the Trip was not yet half over.

13

Looking back now, I think perhaps the six weeks that followed were the most unforgettable of my time with Mr. Churchill.

The Prime Minister planned that after leaving Cairo he would first visit General Eisenhower at Tunis, then fly to Italy to see General Alexander and our front there. But the weather was bad; it was thought possible that a flight across the Mediterranean would be judged unsafe when the time came, and for this reason an alternative method of transport was prepared. Various of the Prime Minister's staff, both male and female, including some Wren Cypher officers, were therefore placed aboard the light cruiser H.M.S. *Penelope* at Alexandria, to proceed to Malta and there to await developments, in case a crossing to Naples by sea became necessary. I was one of these, being considered less airworthy than Peter and Geoffrey. The rest of the party flew off to Tunis. But here plans went awry and events intervened.

We spent a week aboard *Penelope* without being called on for work. It was a joyful interlude in the round of our duties, every minute of which seemed so peaceful and happy that we might not have been at war at all. The girls—there were seven of us—were given officers' cabins two together, the unfortunate owners finding accommodation where they could. I had the Torpedo Officer's cabin to myself, and spent much time in writing up my diary. The crew had had a long spell of service without leave, and seemed delighted with any company which would take their minds off the war and remind them of home; we would sit and chat with them, interested in hearing of their families at home and hoping it did them good to speak of them. They told us about *Penelope* and her famous exploits; how after one particularly severe pounding from the air in Malta Harbour she was renamed H.M.S. *Pepperpot*, because of the number of holes she had acquired. Later she was also called H.M.S. *Porcupine* for a similar reason. She was, they said, unsinkable, and they one and all longed for the next "bit of work" which would bring them into contact with the enemy. Poor *Pepperpot,* she was sunk off Anzio a few weeks later, with the loss of two-thirds of her crew.

The first day at Malta—that island of smells, bells, goats and priests—we were taken around the places of interest there. We saw the damaged dome of Musta, and many black-garbed ladies at their prayers; then on to Rabat, where we bought Maltese lace and from the battlements of the Cathedral gazed out across the island, even catching a glimpse of Sicily sixty miles northward, which our guide told us was possible on about six days in a year. That evening we sat on deck watching a Mickey Rooney movie; but the sight of the damaged buildings standing up starkly white in the bright moonlight, with H.M.S. *Spartan* lying just ahead in Grand Harbour, was to me far more distracting.

But then the Captain received an Urgent signal and soon, with a flurry of water astern, we were gliding out of Grand Harbour and off to Bizerta. It seemed all was not well with the Prime Minister.

We remained anchored off Bizerta for the rest of the week, resting and not worrying about what would happen next. Then General Hollis, the head of the Prime Minister's staff aboard, went ashore for a whole day and returned looking very grave. Mr. Churchill was at Carthage, at General Eisenhower's villa, very seriously ill with pneumonia. Italy was off. Everyone was to fly home except him and me, and we were to join the Carthage party. Good-byes were hastily said, messages taken to families in England. The interlude was over. As a parting shot General Hollis was told, "Don't leave the No.10 Baggage behind"—meaning me.

At the White House, Carthage, there was the greatest anxiety. It seemed that the Prime Minister's life hung in the balance. A famous chest specialist, Brigadier Bedford, had been flown in from Cairo to assist Lord Moran, and three nursing sisters. Mrs. Churchill and Ham were due by air from London that afternoon.

For a day or so I did not see the Prime Minister. He was hardly able to dictate, though he still read many of the telegrams that arrived. Sarah had been keeping her father amused by reading him *Pride and Prejudice,* for he always enjoyed Jane Austen. General Alexander, who had flown over from Italy, was hanging about the office, rather impatient to be gone, one judged. This was the first time I had seen him; he was a very fine figure, and impressed one immediately as being a man of unusual personality. He waited until Mr. Churchill was well enough for them to have a good discussion, then flew back to his scene of operations.

It was not long before it became obvious that Mr. Churchill was on the mend, greatly to the relief of everyone. Work began again as usual. The first time I went in for dictation he said, "Hullo, Miss Layton, how are …", but then realizing that perhaps in reply I might ask, "Rather, how are you, Mr. Churchill?", and the time of day would pass, he quickly checked the question and started on the work. He looked much as usual; I think the arrival of Mrs. Churchill had helped.

Ham and I had a happy reunion. During this time we slept in a villa belonging to General Bedell Smith some distance off, as accommodation at the White House was limited. The kindness and hospitality of the Americans could not have been exceeded. A third Private Secretary, Mr. Colville, had flown out with Mrs. Churchill, and as Geoffrey Green had returned to London, Peter and I had our work cut out to see to the P.M. and the three P.S.'s.

Christmas was spent at Carthage. Never shall I forget that beautiful bay, the blue water, the pink sunrises and sunsets. On Christmas morning a small patrol vessel, which had been on guard each day in the bay, put up a stream of flags which, we were told, in Naval parlance meant "Happy Christmas". Mr. Churchill was much pleased, and was cross when for security reasons the little ship was ordered to haul them down.

And here, oddly enough, for the third time a Private Secretary became engaged. Mr. Brown, our newest and youngest, an ex-Guards Officer, kept saying he was sure that a friend of his, a Free French girl, was somewhere in the neighbourhood, nursing at a Field Station. On Christmas Day he obtained leave and went off in search of her. After many hours he found her, and brought her back to the office as his fiancée. It was all very exciting.

We had a big conference at Carthage, too, at Christmastime. General Alexander flew back from Italy, Generals Eisenhower and Bedell Smith were on the spot, General "Jumbo" Maitland-Wilson, Admiral John Cunningham and Air-Marshal Tedder came from Cairo. There was a party after the conference, and Peter and I were invited; I have recorded rather dolefully that we were able to spare only ten minutes each from our office work! Mr. Churchill was still in complete control of the British Cabinet and war affairs, and all documents and directives between him and London had to pass through the narrow bottleneck of Peter and myself. It kept us extremely busy—in fact, it was a most peculiar Christmas.

One day I did manage to snaffle a car and driver and tour the local "sights". We went to the famous amphitheatre, where more than two thousand years ago plays were performed; its acoustic properties remain to this day. Then to the museum, where I saw the few relics of Carthage and its culture before the Sack. Finally to the Lions' Den, where Christians were martyred—there was the cave where the lions were kept behind bars, the cage in which the Christians were imprisoned, and the trough where the two met at last.

Some days after Christmas we moved again. It was obvious that Mr. Churchill could not yet return to the mists and damp of an English winter, and General Eisenhower therefore put at his disposal a beautiful villa at Marrakesh in Morocco, taken over by the American Army. Before leaving, Mr. Churchill dictated a Press communiqué, addressed principally to the people of Britain, in which he told them that with the help of M. & B. (Moran and Bedford according to him) he had made a wonderful recovery from pneumonia, and was now going to Marrakesh to convalesce. He also said that as he had with him a "highly efficient nucleus staff" he had been able to remain in full control of the Government. When Peter and I saw that bit we looked at one another grinning, and said, "Lord, if he only knew…", remembering the many grumbles we'd had together at the seemingly never-ending stream of telegrams, and the highly inefficient way we sometimes acted at the end of a long day.

At Marrakesh Ham and I really did feel we were in heaven. We shared a room at the well-known Mamounia Hotel, on the first floor, facing east towards the beautiful Snow Atlas Mountains, which tower up thousands of feet. All day and night we could hear the faint beating of drums and far-off wailing. The days were hot and sunny, the nights chilly, clear and bright. When we arose in the early morning the sky would be still pitch-black, full of brilliant stars with perhaps Venus shining through the open balcony door, the air icy cold. Then the line of the mountaintops would become clearer, so that a jet-black ridge stood out from a russet sky behind. The palm trees, some high like feather dusters, some the pineapple shape, would be still as death. The cocks would crow, a few dogs bark, somewhere a native would be beating a drum. Then within a few minutes the sky would grow light, pink clouds would appear—and suddenly the sun would roll over the mountain ridge and day would be here.

The Taylor Villa, where we both spent the days and I half the nights, was what you might call "fantastic". It was built in the Moroccan style, but with every modern convenience and luxury. The furnishings were colourful and Eastern, everything seemed to be red and green or red and gold. The floors were coloured stone mosaic, which made every footfall a clatter. A fairly large staff gradually became established here—the three Private Secretaries, a detachment from the Map Room, Mrs. Hill, who flew out from London, and various folk from other offices. Lord Beaverbrook arrived, and his rather snarly voice could be heard around the courtyard. General Alexander also arrived. Plans for the Anzio landing were being formulated.

One morning, on early duty, I was sent by Mr. Churchill with a query to Commander Thompson. As I knew he must have gone very late to bed and would not yet have arisen, I knocked on his door and, anticipating the customary grunt, opened it and stuck my head within to make my inquiry. But alas, it was not Commander Thompson who peered at me across the bedclothes, but a surprised and rather anxious face, easily recognizable by its sharp-cut features; General Montgomery had unexpectedly arrived late the previous evening. Confused,

I withdrew. Afterwards his A.D.C. told me the General was quite upset at this sudden intrusion.

I always admired his charming and ready smile and the decisive tones of his voice, but saw too little of him to be able to appreciate his undoubted capabilities. To me General Alexander was the real military hero of those times; he spoke with real authority—obviously his brain was as outstanding as his personality. To my not very well-informed mind, General Alexander ranked second only to The Boss.

It was an instructive three weeks at Marrakesh. During the latter part of our stay, when the two Generals had left, Mr. Churchill and his family, with Lord Beaverbrook, Lord Moran, General Hollis and the Private Secretaries, would sometimes drive to the Atlas Mountains for a picnic in the midday sun, to strengthen the Prime Minister. And then we who were left behind would visit the Medina, the native quarter of Marrakesh. There we saw crowds and crowds of dirty, unkempt, ill-clad, underfed Arabs, watching a snake-charmer or listening to a story-teller, or just wandering about doing nothing. We saw fat native women feeding their babies, blind beggars, filthy old men with handbells selling drinking water from gourds suspended at the waist, great-grandfathers with long grey beards and skull-caps, semi-nude children, etc. We bargained at the markets and bought samples of Moroccan leatherwork, sniffed at the spices which were for sale and investigated the rather overwhelming perfumes offered.

I had several letters from my Naval Lieutenant while we were there, and perhaps in the intervals between spells of work I thought of him a few times. When we were home again, after some while Michael came to see me at No.10. He had shaved off his beard—and horrors, he looked so young! It ended there and then; it must have been just a sea trip on the Mediterranean that started it.

Before this period came to an end there was an interesting event. General de Gaulle came to visit the Prime Minister for discussions and asked him to be the guest of honour at a Free French parade. Of course, we had seen the General frequently at Chequers. But it was not until he visited us at Marrakesh that I had the opportunity of trying on his General's cap (while he was talking to the P.M.). I was surprised at its smallness and how it perched on top of my hair; for such a tall man he must have a positively minute head. Mrs. Churchill conversed with him in perfect French; Mr. Churchill with great fluency and far less accuracy, and a very funny accent.

The parade was really worth seeing. There were dozens of romantically garbed sheiks, local bigwigs and French Generals seated on a wooden platform, in front of which was a saluting-base. Here the two Heads of States soon appeared. Then came the march-past. First there were Senegalese troops on foot—black as pitch, in reddish uniforms with red fezzes and bayonets on their rifles, hopelessly out of step but obviously tough soldiers. Fighters roared low overhead. Next came the Foreign Legion, also on foot. They looked as though throat-cutting before breakfast was their usual form. Then the Spahis, coal-black, mounted, wearing blue pantaloons, red jackets, white turbans and cloaks, clattering past straight as pokers in their saddles. By now bombers were racing overhead, uncomfortably low. Last came a parade of armour. During all this time the two Great Men stood together on the saluting-base, acknowledging salutes and giving the V-sign at intervals.

During the latter part of our time at Marrakesh, further Visitors arrived. Mr. Harold Macmillan, at that time Minister Resident at Algiers, and Mr. Duff Cooper, British Ambassador to the Free French, with Lady Diana. Brigadier Fitzroy Maclean turned up in greatest secrecy, soon to be dropped again by parachute into Yugoslavia; he wore a kilt, and we thought him very good-looking. Another guest at the villa was El Glaoui of Marrakesh, the local Big Noise, whom Mr. Churchill had known before the war.

Most of these needed secretarial help. Our favourite was Mr. Macmillan, who was pleasantly friendly and approachable. With the addition of Mrs. Hill to our numbers we were well able to cope with this, and were not unduly pressed for time.

Halfway through January came the time to leave. We were flown to Gibraltar, and there embarked in the battleship H.M.S. *King George V.* which was waiting to take us home.

It was a new experience to travel in a battleship. It seemed like a floating city, and we were glad to see notices for our benefit: "This Way Forward", "To the Wardroom", etc., which must have infuriated the proper inhabitants. Ham and I shared a vast cabin astern; it seemed right over the propellers, and the shaking and roaring was continuous. The office was a little farther forward, but the Prime Minister's quarters were just under the bridge and miles on towards the bow. To walk there took at least ten minutes. Four flights of steps had to be mounted, and the continual up-draught was an embarrassment to one's skirts, particularly as Royal Marines were stationed on duty at every turn.

Our last day aboard was a Sunday, and we attended service in the Ship's Chapel, again singing "Eternal Father". Then, that evening, off on to Plymouth docks and into our special train, and soon we were London-bound.

Our arrival at Paddington Station was delayed until a reasonable hour the following morning, when, as always on our return from a trip, the entire Cabinet, the Service Chiefs and various others turned up at the station to welcome the Prime Minister home. Their greetings on this occasion were particularly sincere, after his long absence and severe illness. A crowd of well-known personalities milled around the carriage door. Mr. Churchill, wearing his reefer jacket and yachting cap (his favourite outfit), his cigar well lit and a large beam lighting up his face, moved happily among his colleagues. It was nice to be home again.

For me, there was little opportunity to digest all I had learned; to think of the strange and exciting places I had seen and stayed in, of the people I had met and the different ways of life I had peeped at. Nowadays, standing back to look at all that happened, I can feel the rare privilege it was to be there at that time.

14

Perhaps it was rather hard to settle down once more. But we had the knowledge of great things to come, and personally at this time I did not feel very happy when away from the office. Our war in Italy was prospering slowly but surely; our air offensive against Germany increased daily; the Russians were rolling the Germans backward; and … we all knew that D-Day was not far off.

In the early months of 1944 the German night-raiders returned. Some severe damage was caused, particularly by the incendiary bombs, so that it was called the Fire Blitz. This was the cause of the following event.

I was on late duty and we were all at No.10, for the Prime Minister had important guests to dinner and was entertaining them in the two small rooms below the Cabinet Room. Presently the sirens announced that our evening visitors had arrived; some while later came the "Overhead" signal, and Mr. Martin, who was on duty, ordered his own shorthand-writer, one Liz Gilliatt, and me to retire to the shelter. I felt a wee bit indignant; never before had I sheltered. But at the shelter door we were met by Mr. Churchill, who hurried us within and directed us to scramble on to an upper bunk in the first of the two small rooms. Mrs. Hill, Ham, Mrs. Landemare (the cook) and her two little kitchen-maids were already seated about the walls. Through the doorway a few feet off we had an excellent view of the Prime Minister and his guests, who had also retired to the shelter; they sat on chairs, stools or bunks in the second small room. They were the members of the War Cabinet and—His Majesty the King!

Of course, I had seen the King on a number of occasions; he quite frequently came to dine with the Prime Minister; but I had never listened to him talking before. We sat there for over an hour, our eyes goggling and our ears flapping, our legs dangling over the edge of the bunk. It was intensely interesting to see what happened when The Great got together for a purely social occasion. Actually, it was just like any gang of friends sitting down to pass a pleasant evening. The King seemed boyishly eager to join in with the others, and told one or two funny stories, which made one feel that in addition to being King he was a very nice person indeed. Mr. Oliver Lyttelton, always a wag, related a few anecdotes with imitations: the conversation was not businesslike at all! Poor Mr. Martin, struggling with the telephone to find out what was happening, looked quite distracted at the continuous roars of laughter. The raid was particularly heavy that night, and the Prime Minister kept dodging in and out of the shelter door to see if the rest of the place was still standing. At intervals other members of the party—Mr. Attlee or Mr. Bevin or Mr. Eden—would stroll across to make a joking remark to us in the anteroom; I hope they didn't think we were nervous—we had forgotten all about the air raid.

When at last it was safe for the guests to leave, we had a charming smile and "Good night" from His Majesty as he passed us. We had planned to jump down from the upper bunk and stand straight as soon as he moved, but unfortunately the little kitchen-maids were just then scrambling out of the lower bunks, so we merely sat tight and smiled back. But next day I fear Liz Gilliatt and I spread ourselves somewhat among the less fortunate in the office: even for such hardened types as ourselves that was a memorable evening.

It must, I think, have been at about this time that the position of the personal staff was eased greatly by the part-time addition of two young women, Marian and Jo. They did one night duty each per week in town, and went alternate weekends to Chequers with us—Marian with me and Jo with Mrs. Hill. From that time onward we didn't really have any grumbles about lack of staff.

It was, of course, now my regular task, on my alternate weekends on duty, to travel with the Prime Minister in the car to and from Chequers whenever he wished to dictate, which was now more often than not. Sometimes he would be in a communicative mood, and would make little remarks as we drove along: "Look at those little lambs jumping about in that field!"—"What are those yellow flowers growing over there?"—"How fast are we going?—must be nearly sixty." Naturally one felt honoured. But I would make little or no answer, telling myself over and over again: "Hold hard, keep quiet; better be thought a near deaf-mute than incur a reprimand for wasting his time with unnecessary remarks or pointless replies."

So often in these days the journey back to London would be the occasion for the first draft of one of Mr. Churchill's speeches or statements; perhaps the fact of being alone in the car, free from interruptions, produced the right mood. I was always fascinated to watch what I felt was the preview of his delivery. His hands, which were small and beautifully moulded, would indicate that his thoughts were taking shape; and then the words would come pouring out, one subject following another and being dealt with in orderly precision. It seemed impossible for him to dictate in a flat, matter-of-fact way—he always put the force of his feelings into what he said.

Mr. Churchill seemed to have a wide knowledge of the poets, and could always produce a quotation to illustrate a point he wished to make. These he would sometimes later cut out of his statement. But when on reaching the office we would check them in our reference book of quotations, we were often surprised to note how nearly word-perfect he was.

The months before the invasion were a strain on us all. Hours were later than usual, tempers shorter. If the knowledge was a burden to us, it must have been an oppression to those who bore the responsibility. There was by this time no anxiety, in my own mind at least, that I might accidentally betray any secrets, or indeed anything at all. Every part of my work was locked away in one side of my brain and had no relation to any outside life that time allowed. The others agreed on this: one felt oneself two persons, the person one was to oneself and the person one presented to other people. But I certainly never met anyone at this time who seemed in any way anxious to find anything out; the attitude was rather, "We know you can't talk about your work, so let's talk about something else."

In the office we tried very hard not to give Mr. Churchill any cause for impatience. We understood, indeed, how his whole being was bound up in the impending landings and the battles that would follow, and we laid ourselves out to avoid any of those petty irritations which tiredness or lack of 100 per cent concentration might have caused. The Private Secretaries, too, gave of their best. One of them, Mr. Peck, had an exceptionally fast brain, as perhaps the following incident will serve to illustrate.

One morning, as Mr. Churchill sat in bed working at his precious Box but pausing sometimes to lean back deep in thought, puffing away meanwhile on the usual huge cigar, I observed that he was in a somewhat edgy mood. Presently he stretched out for the little white telephone by his bed, which connected directly to the Private Secretary in the office not far off. Mr. Peck was on duty that morning, and when he answered, Mr. Churchill merely said gruffly into the mouthpiece "Gimme the moon", and replaced the receiver. I wondered what would be the reaction in the office, but soon Mr. Peck entered bearing the chart of the moon's phases for the month of June, invasion month. This was received without comment, and was indeed what was required. I thought to myself, "Lucky for you, John Peck, that you could read his thoughts so well."

One felt the whole nation knew the time was near. Purpose and resolve seemed tighter. Queues were longer, but one did not hear the customary grumbles. Travel became even more impossible, but no comments were made or questions asked about the masses of men and armour moving southward and congregating there. I felt the deepest admiration for the way the British people faced up to the prospect of the struggle to come—"grim and gay" never suited them better. They said it was difficult to know what to talk about to one's friends—food was always a safe and popular topic, or what the newspapers said; otherwise one stuck to the past and the future (oh, the future, when it was all over) and avoided discussion of the present.

The roads were full of military traffic. One Monday morning, returning from Chequers, the Prime Minister's car became caught between two convoys travelling in opposite directions. We kept swinging out into the road to pass a DUCK-bearing truck before swinging in to meet the next Army lorry. Mr. Churchill seemed unaffected, but by the time London was reached I felt very sick indeed and was only grateful that the worst had not happened in the car.

The weekend before D-day was spent in our special train at a tiny siding outside Southampton. It was not particularly convenient or comfortable, but Mr. Churchill felt he had to be there on the spot. The train stood high in a cutting. The Prime Minister had brought various Cabinet Ministers and advisers—General Smuts, Mr. Ernest Bevin and others—to share his vigil, and as the office was separated from the sleeping and dining quarters by the coach in which they all sat, Marian and I (who were on duty that weekend) were forced to lower ourselves about seven feet to the track, trot along and scramble up again every time it was necessary to make the journey. Mr. Churchill went off one day to inspect the forces in their last preparations, and returned with that dogged look on his face that betokened great emotion. The thought of the lives which would so soon be snuffed out was more awful and serious than can be described. It was hard to sleep that night.

Late on the Sunday we heard that owing to weather, the time of setting out had been put back twenty-four hours. Anti-climax. We returned to the Annexe. The following night the programme took place, with results which are well known.

Less than a week after the invading forces crossed the coast of France, flying-bombs began to arrive in Britain. We had long known that such a form of attack was being prepared—since the days of the First Quebec Conference, when the name Peenemunde had first come into prominence—and from the first they seemed far more demoralizing than piloted aircraft had ever been. I quote an extract from an account I wrote to my mother at the time:

"A flying-bomb travels at considerable speed, though not so fast as a fighter aircraft, and when seen from below looks rather like some horrid, vindictive little mosquito dodging through the clouds. It lets forth a growling roar which is unmistakable for anything else—a loud, unpleasant sound discernible even above the noise of air-conditioning and typewriters, or the traffic in Piccadilly Circus on a blowy, gusty day. As long as the noise goes on you know you are safe, but when it stops you must duck, for then the engine stops and the bomb dives at an angle for the ground. If you hear the sound overhead, you know the bomb is already well past you, but if it stops as it is still approaching, you must listen for the whistle and say your prayers. If you don't hear the whistle, your number is probably up, for they say you never hear the one that hits you.

"If you are outside and the Overhead sounds, you usually keep walking and look for a nice solid-looking doorway to dodge into. Before you cross a Street you think to yourself, 'If IT suddenly popped over the roof-tops and I were in the middle, should I have time to dash to St. Martin's-in-the-Fields *if* the engine stopped?' Then you hear the familiar crumbly roar, so you wait by your doorway thinking to yourself, 'Praise de Lawd and keep de engine runnin'.' And when you see *it,* travelling straight and fast through the clouds, you walk calmly and rather cold-bloodedly on, knowing you are safe from that one anyway."

These nasty things would come over in batches of six or eight, usually three or four times during the night and once or twice in the daytime. When at home at the flat, I sometimes watched them from the fourth-floor window—during daylight merely wicked black specks, at night the jet exhaust making a light so that they looked like shooting stars. Often, as one was on night duty, sitting in the P.M.'s study, a Map Room officer would come in to say that six "flies" were on their way to London. Sometimes there would be a far-off bump. Sometimes they would come very close, cutting off just before they reached us, and frequently the windows would have blown in without the steel shutters, which a Marine orderly always closed when the alarm was given.

Usually Mr. Churchill took no notice of these disturbances, or made a joking remark to help morale. One night when there was a particularly heavy crash, he looked up from the paper he was studying. "Aren't you afraid?" he asked. "Don't you want to go to the shelter?" I grinned broadly and said, "No, thank you." "But aren't you afraid the whole building is going to collapse on top of us?" I felt there was something of a twinkle behind this, and merely said again, "No, thank you." Once or twice afterwards he said, "I know you aren't afraid of the bombs." I didn't deserve any praise for this: perhaps I *was* scared inside, but I can't imagine what he would have thought of me if I had chosen to go to the shelter while he remained above ground.

One Sunday morning we were at Chequers, and in the office the Private Secretary on duty (it was Mr. Peck) was talking on the telephone to Mr. Rowan, who was on duty at the Annexe. Over the wire Mr. Peck could hear the rattle of a flying bomb (or doodlebug, as they were called), and Mr. Rowan said, "Yes, coming quite near, I think"—then "Good Heavens", and the line went dead as he dived under the desk. When he got up again he told Mr. Peck the window had blown in, and outside not far off he could see a great dust rising. The bomb had fallen on the Guards Chapel in Birdcage Walk, and many Sunday worshippers were killed. The Prime Minister was much upset by this incident.

In general it seemed that this new form of torture was having a bad effect on the people. Everyone was determinedly cheerful and wouldn't admit to any feeling of apprehension, but no one looked very happy. Many who had withstood the Blitz following the Battle of Britain began evacuating to the country. The office char, a tough East-Ender who had always made light of "Jerry", seemed to be in for a nervous breakdown. It was, of course, the effect of five years of war and indifferent food.

It *was* a difficult time. The war seemed to have been going on for a lifetime. Try as one would, the constant late hours and nerve strain had their effect. Mr. Churchill was particularly busy with many speeches, including an enormously long review of the war in the House of Commons. It was just one thing after another.

We all knew Mr. Churchill's saying "A change is as good as a rest"—a maxim which I imagine he has imposed upon himself and his staff for most of his life. Rest was out of the question unless one gave in altogether. I longed to get away—for a change, another trip, anything which would get me out of the trough of feeling I could go on no longer. I remember walking in the sunken rose-garden at Chequers and reading on the sundial:

> *Ye Houres do fly*
> *Full Soone we die.*
> *in age Secure*
> *Ye House and Ye Hills*
> *Alone Endure.*

and thinking to myself "Hear, Hear."

But then relief came. In September we went to Canada again.

The Second Quebec Conference did not have the glitter and magnitude of the First; nevertheless, it was a most welcome break and also an opportunity to stock up one's system with Food—Food, of which one sometimes dreamed.

We travelled both ways by the *Queen Mary* again, but stayed less than a week in Quebec. There was one unforgettable morning in the Atlantic *en route,* when sixty-five aircraft from a nearby British carrier flew out in salute to the Prime Minister, diving, wheeling, rolling and finally flying in stately formation low over the ship. We found the little town of Quebec still suffering from the events of our visit the year before, when extensive buying had taken place; the shops were empty, and our demands in the stocking line could not be fulfilled.

On the way home there was bad news. The battles at Arnhem and at the Nijmegen Salient had developed, and it was heartbreaking to hear each day of the losses of our fine Airborne Division. We came home refreshed but in a serious mood.

15

It was, I think, at about this time that we first knew rockets had fallen in the British Isles. For a few weeks no official announcement was made, though it was obvious that the public had their suspicions of these unexplained and very noisy explosions. You would be sitting quietly at your desk at No.10, deep in a pile of papers, when without the least warning there would come a terrific explosion and a blast which caused the building to shiver. You would look rather sheepishly at your fellows and say with a sickly smile, "Guess what that was …", and they would grin and reply, "Just another gas main blowing up, of course." These pleasant creatures did not worry us as the flying-bombs had, because by the time they had arrived the damage was done, but for the victims, chiefly in London's East End, they were most terrifying.

During October Mr. Churchill flew again to Moscow. Peter's health was none too good—he was tired—and so on this occasion the office staff was to consist of Mr. Martin and three Young Women—Sheila, who was an expert on official documents, Marian and me. Moscow!—Heavens—*Moscow*!

We took off from Northolt at 1 a.m. and breakfasted at Naples, where the Prime Minister conferred with General Maitland-Wilson, then Commander-in-Chief of the Mediterranean Theatre (we called him C.-in-C. Med.), and General Alexander. Thereafter we flew south, over Sorrento and Capri, past Stromboli, across the Mediterranean over Benghazi, and so to Cairo, where we had dinner. About 1 a.m. we again took off, and at noon the following day reached Moscow.

A rather queer-looking ceremony was taking place as our aircraft (the third) touched down. A smart Guard of Honour had turned out to meet the Prime Minister and was at that moment marching past him, a high-stepping march rather like the goose-step, which flapped their long coats up and down. It was cold and windy, everyone looked frozen. All our party, as they arrived in turn, were being frantically photographed by Soviet Secret Service men with motion-picture cameras, so that our features could later be scanned for any sign of a suspicious countenance.

Thereafter we were driven through Moscow to the Dacha or country house of M. Molotov, some twenty miles the other side of the city. Here we lived in great luxury for the best part of two weeks. We worked hard, as always, but oh, the thrill and delight it was to be in this strange country, so long the object of our interest!

The Dacha was a two-storey building surrounded by a wooden palisade, guarded, of course, at the front gate. It was not an impressive-looking house, but comfortable inside. We three were accommodated in a wing by ourselves. We were much impressed by the service from the Russian maidens, one of whom was always in attendance to scrub one's back when bathing. They made our beds in such a queer way, too, folding the sheets and blankets all together with the corners underneath, so that when once beneath them one had to keep still or everything fell off—one couldn't get *into* bed. We were told the reason for this was that Russian people have a trapped feeling if tucked into bed.

Russian hospitality was quite overwhelming. The food was as one might imagine it to have been in Czarist days. They might have been trying to impress us with their wealth. At breakfast, which was served about 9 o'clock, we were encouraged to eat enough to last for the rest of the day—starting with caviar and vodka, then smoked salmon, cold meats, cheese, pickles, etc., to be followed by omelettes which must have been made with twelve eggs apiece, pies, bread, butter—nothing was left out. Luncheon and dinner usually lasted two hours each. Each meal would be of about ten courses. We could not convince our waiters that all we wanted was a quick snack. When once Marian refused a course the waiter burst into tears, and thinking he might be going to lose his head as a consequence, she quickly changed her mind. In case it be thought I am exaggerating, here is one of our menus:

    Caviar, with brown bread and butter, tomatoes, cucumbers,
        radishes, shredded beetroot, toast
    Smoked salmon and smoked turbot
    Bismarck herring
    Sliced ham and tongue
    Sucking pig with creamed horseradish sauce
    Jellied caviar
    Russian salad
    Hot mushrooms in butter
    Soup
    Grilled turbot with boiled potatoes
    Roast chicken

Steamed cauliflower with butter sauce
Ice-cream "bomb"
Dessert (apples, pears, peaches, grapes)
Coffee

Each course was served separately on clean plates, with some delay between, during which we were pressed to consume much vodka, white wine and red wine, and finally cognac and liqueur vodka. We used to wonder, while we still had sense to do so, who did the washing-up and where all the crockery was kept.

The Prime Minister had brought with him a number of advisers. The Foreign Secretary was there and various Foreign Office experts; also the C.I.G.S. and some odd Generals; General Ismay; and, of course, Lord Moran. These with their staffs were based at the British Embassy in Moscow—we saw little of them.

Every day Mr. Churchill would make the journey into Moscow to talk with Marshal Stalin, returning to the Dacha late in the afternoon. One day there was to be a banquet in his honour, at 2 o'clock in the afternoon. As he was leaving the Dacha, he suddenly announced that he wanted to dictate in the car, so with scarcely a minute in which to fix my appearance, I accompanied him.

Driving through the pleasant autumn woods, which reminded me somewhat of British Columbia, he dictated a document for Mr. Stalin's immediate consideration. I was to go to the Embassy and type it out, and thereafter could have a look around Moscow as long as I was back at the Embassy at 4.30. He was disembarked at the Hall in Spiridonievka Street, which name to me had an interesting sound. He was looking very smart in his khaki uniform (which was the official dress of the Lord Warden of the Cinque Ports, one of his offices), and as he went off he turned to smile good-bye. I knew he understood that being driven off by a Russian driver through the streets of Moscow to a place whose whereabouts I didn't know might be alarming, and he wanted me to know it was all right. As we drove away I thought, "Amazing man, he knows *everything*." As soon as his paper was typed out it was delivered to him at the banquet.

As can be imagined, it was a very interesting afternoon. The Ambassador's Private Secretary was good enough to accompany me; one could not have gone alone. Very soon there was a short, dark man with a slouch hat following us, a member of the N.K.V.D. or political police. I saw the Kremlin, on the bank of the Moscow River, opposite the Embassy, and what a strange collection of buildings it seemed, some domed and some square-roofed, some covered with weird and ornate pompoms, some with spires, two churches looking like enormous cockle-shells. To the right of this gathering was the Church of St. Basil, so oddly shaped that one expected to see gnomes and goblins peeping around the towers. There is a story that Czar Ivan the Terrible, for whom it was built, was so pleased with his church that he had the eyes of the architect put out, lest any other potentate bribe the latter into building a similar pile.

Nearby was Red Square and Lenin's Tomb, a great square mass connected to the Kremlin by an underground passage, so that on parade days the Marshal could easily reach the top of the tomb to take the salute. The town, which had wide, dusty streets and squares as big as lakes, was comparatively empty of people. Such as were about were very poorly dressed, the women in dark grey with grey shawls about their heads, thick woollen socks and split shoes, or no shoes, the men nearly all in tattered uniforms.

We went down the Underground, which seemed extraordinarily modern, clean, electrified and well-run compared with the rest of Moscow. And into the Moscow Hotel, of considerable magnificence and obviously designed to impress the visitor; here were soft lights and thick carpets, a few shops (not that one would have dreamt of buying anything at those prices), statues of Lenin and Stalin. Then back to the Embassy, through the pink-clouded sunset.

The banquet continued until 6.30, after which the Prime Minister picked me up at the Embassy and dictated all the way back to the Dacha. This was, I felt, a tribute to his powers of "taking it". Later I was able to see the document I had typed, now with the signatures of two Heads of States at the foot. The signatures were somewhat scratchy, and I gathered that this particular piece of business had been attended to rather late in the proceedings.

The Soviet officer in charge at the Dacha told us an amusing story which was, he said, typical of Russia. There was a time when some officers were sent on duty to the Ural Mountains, and to pass away the evenings they invented a game called "Tiger is Coming". The dining-table would be set for one less officer than was to be present—that is, if there were to be nine officers, eight places would be laid. One officer would then leave the room, the rest would get under the table and the glasses all round would be filled with vodka. The absent officer would then return, saying "Tiger is Coming", drink up all the glasses of vodka and sit down at one of the places. This was a signal for the rest to spring up from beneath the table and scramble for a place. The one left without would then leave the room, the rest would get under the table again, the glasses would be refilled and the process repeated. At last a stage would be reached when someone failed to spring from beneath the table but remained on the floor, whereupon one of the places would be removed—and so on till but one place and one valiant officer remained above the boards. He would, of course, be pronounced the Tiger.

Occasionally we felt our hosts might be trying to make Tigers of us!

For a few days towards the end of our stay Mr. Churchill remained in Moscow, at a house in Ostrovskaya Street set aside for important visitors, as he found the journeying took up too much time. This was an elegant and comfortable spot but small, with sleeping accommodation for only Mr. Martin, Lord Moran and Sawyers, besides the P.M. That meant that we three girls had to travel from the Dacha into Moscow early and back late, which was wearing, but at least by varying our hours of duty we were able to see something of the city, as well as of the Russian Ballet and Opera, a superb treat. When we arrived back at the Dacha in the early hours, the Russian officer in charge there, who spoke English perfectly, would be waiting up for us with caviar, vodka and fruit laid out in case we felt in need of refreshment. There seemed no limit to Soviet hospitality … but we were very careful about the vodka!

One morning as I was on duty beside Mr. Churchill while he worked in his room at the Town House, I was reminded of our morning troubles at the Annexe. It always upset his mental processes if any persistent or unusual noise could be heard, and this morning was just unfortunate. First, the Russian guards on duty at the front door, not far from the bedroom, were chatting to each other. I hurried to quiet them by gestures—the poor frightened little men seemed horrified at their offence. Next, the public address system which is in every street was switched on, and Moscow at large was treated to the efforts of a trembling soprano. "What on earth is that howling?" asked Mr. Churchill, none too pleased. I explained there was nothing to be done about it, and luckily it soon quieted down. Not long afterwards Mr. Martin, telephoning in the office opposite, was obliged to shout on account of a bad connection. The Prime Minister looked up—"Who *is* that jawing away out there?" I flew to shut the office door. But that was not all. Somebody in the house adjoining started hammering—*hammering*! After one glance at The Countenance, I left the room without a word and implored the housekeeper to do something about the trouble. Eventually there was peace.

Another morning we had similar trouble. The inoffensive little guard at the front door had a cough. After bearing this rather impatiently for some while, Mr. Churchill suddenly roared at me, "Go and fetch that secretary chap", so I hastily went for the officer in charge of the household, who spoke perfect English, preparing him for the worst. However, I should have known better. There was a quick change of front. The Prime Minister said solicitously, "There is a *poor* man at the door who has a *very* bad cough. I feel he ought to be put on duty where there is less draught, otherwise it might turn to pneumonia."

Sometimes I used to wonder whether life would be the same working for a different man in the same circumstances. I used to imagine, instead, the mild Mr. Attlee, or even the charming Mr. Eden. Would it be the same interesting, unpredictable existence? *Never.*

Almost every evening in Moscow salvoes would be fired to announce the recapture of a new city by Soviet troops. As these started we would hurry outside to watch the showers of red, green and yellow stars which went with each salvo. The luxury with which we were surrounded tended to make us forget the struggles of the Russian people, who were totally at war in a way in which even the British had never been. Many buildings in Moscow showed signs of German shellfire. The poverty of the people, the bread queues, the impossible prices of the few goods in the shops were a reminder that the war had not been easy for these people.

One evening we had a great treat. A Command Performance was given at the Bolshoi Theatre, attended by Mr. Churchill and Marshal Stalin, and seats were offered to all visitors. We watched the first act of *Giselle;* then heard some solo arias from well-known Russian singers. In the interval the crowd that filled the theatre gave a terrific welcome to the two great men, who sat together in the centre box. They stood and shook hands, amid roaring applause. The second half was the Red Army choir, who gave a thrilling performance topped off with some wild and lively Cossack dances. Numbers of young men came springing forth and danced furiously about, going almost mad with glee; they fought, they leapt, jumped, spun, kicked and pranced, till one longed to fling oneself in and dance with them. It was a wonderful performance.

The next afternoon the Prime Minister gave us a fright by developing a sudden temperature. He was put to bed, and we all felt miserable. The others, even Mr. Martin, had arranged to see *Swan Lake* that evening, so I was on my own after dinner, and presently he asked me to read to him. For an hour and a half, therefore, I sat by his bedside reading a perfectly dreadful book called *A Primer of the Coming World,* about the influence of capitalism on wars, feeling how inadequate was my brainpower since I could understand not a word of what I was reading. He sat with a black bandage over his eyes, concentrating, occasionally saying "A wee bit faster", or "Slacken off a little", to show he was not asleep. Fortunately, the fever did not develop; next day he was better.

I do not think much was gained at this meeting. The chief subject was Poland, and we went home with no agreement signed, which was a pity. However, there was a heart-warming feeling of comradeliness.

The time for leaving had come. We three girls were somewhat tired by a succession of nights of three hours in bed. Nowadays, when I read my diary, I think we must have had superhuman energy. There was no longer any interest in seeing sights—all we wanted was sleep.

The Prime Minister told me to travel in his aircraft, as he wished to dictate on the journey, and just before we left Moscow Central airport I was aboard the York with only Mr. Churchill, Marshal Stalin, Mr. Eden and M. Molotov, while good-byes were said (in which I did *not* participate). M. Molotov looked just as his pictures had led one to imagine—inscrutable and slit-eyed behind his glasses. Marshal Stalin was much shorter than I had thought, and the twinkle in his eye looked, somehow, all too knowing. Bundled up in his long Army greatcoat, he reminded me of a rather wicked-looking stuffed doll.

Off we flew, and then occurred the most memorable of my own adventures.

We were to fly across the Mediterranean to Cairo, as the Turks would not allow us to use their air, and in view of this long hop and the importance of the cargo, the aircraft were to be serviced as well as refuelled in the Crimea. Accordingly, we came down near a tiny place called Simferopol. The Germans had left these parts only four or five months previously and, having scorched the earth, had left ruin and desolation behind them. However, a small house in Simferopol had been put in order as a resting-place for the Prime Minister and the principals of his party, and during the afternoon they congregated there. Besides Mr. Churchill there were Mr. Eden, Sir Alan Brooke, General Ismay, Lord Moran, General Jacob, and various Foreign Office and War Office advisers, as well as the P.M.'s staff of Mr. Martin, Detective-Inspector Hughes, Sawyers and myself. That evening they were to be entertained to a banquet, the trappings of which had been flown from Moscow that day; the hosts were to be the Mayor of the Soviet of Crimea and one General Yermetchenko of the Russian Naval Air Force, accompanied by interpreters.

Dinner-time came, and Mr. Churchill said that Inspector Hughes, Sawyers and I must go in to dinner with the main party, there being no separate dining-place for us. Fortunately, we found a small table and sat together.

It was an amazing scene, like something out of Hans Andersen. The room was lit only by candles, and we were served by fresh-faced Russian girls, obviously hastily thrust into waitresses' uniform, wearing unaccustomed high heels on which they tottered round awkwardly. Course succeeded course, the air became wavy with cigar smoke, the candles guttered, the vodka flowed. Looking around at the scene I thought, "This could never happen again." Soon toasts and speeches began. There was a toast to The King, then one to Marshal Stalin; one to the Red Air Force, and one in reply to the Royal Air Force. Then I saw Mr. Churchill looking at me with a wicked twinkle, and wondered what was going to happen. He rose to his feet and proposed the health of "Miss Layton, the only lady present", at which all that grand company got good-naturedly to its feet, laughing, and drank the toast. General Yermetchenko seized the flowers out of a bowl on the table and dumped them, dripping, into my lap, by way of a bouquet, and then the company called for a speech. Feeling fairly idiotic and scarlet-faced, I stood up and said, "Thank you very much, I feel greatly honoured", and sat down again hastily, which someone was afterwards kind enough to tell me was "the perfect speech, neither too long nor too short". Soon the after-dinner speeches began in earnest, and very amusing they were.

But the evening was not yet over. When the party left the tables, the gallant General Yermetchenko indicated that he wished me to accompany him to an adjoining room. I felt anxious, wondering what were the after-dinner customs in these parts. I called Inspector Hughes, but the General waved him away. He then indicated that we were to drink to Anglo-Soviet relations, and produced two tumblers of red wine, which on his instructions we drank "bottoms up", I rather innocently thinking I should humour him. However, the tumblers were then refilled, and we "bottomed up" a second time. Fortunately, I was then rescued by Mr. Martin, who put his head round the door and, seeing the party threatening to become a bit merry, decided I had better now return to the aircraft.

That evening made a good story for those in Whitehall, who found the adventures of the Prime Minister's Young Ladies a source of amusement!

Home we went via Cairo, where we stayed one night, and Naples, where the Prime Minister spent some time conferring with Generals Alexander and Maitland-Wilson, and Mr. Harold Macmillan, who was Minister Resident at Caserta (Naples) by this time. I have recorded rather pompously that next day the latter was so kind as to carry my case to the York aircraft and help me step aboard!

16

For a few weeks after returning to London we sat back on the laurels of our latest adventure, but even more was to come.

In November Lord Moyne, Minister of State in the Middle East, was assassinated. It was such a short time since we had left him at the Beit el Azrak, poor man. For Armistice Day the Prime Minister visited Paris and walked down the Champs EIysées with General de Gaulle, the two receiving an immense ovation from the newly-liberated French. Our assault upon the fortress of Germany was in progress. There was a statement by the Prime Minister to the House of Commons warning us "This is just the moment not to slacken—tirelessness is what we have to show now"—oh Lord!

The atmosphere in the office seemed to have mellowed. It was, of course, partly because of the experiences we had all shared and partly because of the lessening of tension regarding the outcome of our affairs. Naturally, full concentration on work was at all times required—inefficiency and slackness simply had no part in our daily routine—but there seemed a warm feeling of confidence and security and comradeship.

Mr. Churchill seemed full of twinkles. Perhaps he was beginning to see the end in sight, at last. Several times he teased me about the Russian General. Once he burst out laughing, and when I looked surprised he said, "I can't help laughing every time I think of you and that bunch of flowers." Despite his seventy years and the fact that the war had been going on for five years, he bore his responsibilities extremely well.

I had long ago realized that my difficulties at the outset of my time with him had been a result of the tremendous weight he carried and also of my own inexperience. Now, while there was a great deal of physical weariness to contend with, there was no longer the same anxiety about serving the Prime Minister. I could write perkily to my mother: "The evening has been spent in dashing in and out of the Study, where He is conferring with four of his advisers, an Admiral of the Fleet, a Field-Marshal, a full General and a Minister—taking down various things and then reading them aloud to the assembled company." One day, dismissing me after dictation, Mr. Churchill said, "You may fall out now. Go and pray for strength to withstand the many trials and tribulations that will undoubtedly fall upon you before you reach the age of ninety-nine." It was one of our happy periods, with the feeling that it could not be very long before the war came to an end.

Early in December Mr. Churchill again addressed the House of Commons. Fierce fighting was taking place in Greece between Government troops with British military backing, and the forces of E.L.A.S., which was the military instrument of the Communist Party there. The latter had descended upon Athens with the object of seizing power and becoming the governing force in Greece. They were not, Mr. Churchill said, entirely self-seeking, but had certainly devoted more time during the years of German occupation to attacking members of the less Left-inclined Greek parties than to making it unpleasant for the occupying Germans.

Bitter fighting took place in Athens as December advanced; our troops were driven back and the R.A.F. Headquarters overrun. The Greek Prime Minister, M. Papandreou, threatened to resign. It looked as though Greece would go Communist if nothing were done.

There were those in the House who considered British intervention in this civil war a mistake; but since we had intervened, we could not now withdraw. Mr. Churchill was extremely unhappy about the situation, which he felt he could resolve if only he were on the spot. The Archbishop of Athens, Archbishop Damaskinos, had stepped forward and looked as though he might prove a leader, but he needed guidance and backing.

The day before Christmas Eve, a Saturday, the Churchill family withdrew to Chequers for the Christmas holiday. Marian and I happened to be on duty. On the morning of Christmas Eve, the Private Secretary (it was Mr. Colville) told me the Prime Minister had it in mind to fly that night to Athens to make a personal attempt to solve the crisis. Excited twittering took place, naturally. All day the subject was debated on the higher level; first he would go, then he was persuaded that he certainly could not, and so on. There were telephone conversations with the Foreign Secretary, and telegrams and signals flashing to and from the British Embassy in Athens. At about 7 p.m. Mr. Churchill decided finally that the trip was on, and that he would take with him Mr. Colville, Mr. Eden and his Private Secretary Mr. Dixon, Lord Moran, one detective, Sawyers, and the two Young Women on duty. (Peter Kinna had been waiting all day at the Annexe with his bag packed, his holiday spoiled, on instructions from the Private Office, who felt that were the trip to take place he would be the most suitable person to be included; he told us afterwards he was so glad to be let off.)

We didn't need telling twice. We flew to pack up all that would be required, and shortly before 1 o'clock on Christmas morning the party took off from Northolt in a beautiful new bird, the first Skymaster to reach Britain, a gift to the Prime Minister from General Arnold, U.S.A. It felt firm, powerful and secure.

About 8 a.m. we landed at Naples, Pomigliano airfield, where we had breakfast, then continued eastward. At the tail of the aircraft was Mr. Churchill's bedroom, and here he could lie and work comfortably with his Box, pencils, klop and tags beside him, very much as he did at home. On such occasions one had to remember to empty his pens, or the change in altitude made the ink squirt out, which produced a Crisis.

About 2 o'clock we circled Athens and the Piraeus, then landed at Kalamaki airfield. The aircraft was at once surrounded by British soldiers, who ushered aboard Field-Marshal Alexander (as he had now become) and Mr. Macmillan, flown there from Caserta, the British Ambassador to Greece, Mr. Leeper, and the British Commander on the spot, General Scobie. It was terribly cold; there was plenty of snow about. We sat huddled in our coats while the principals conferred in the saloon. I saw Inspector Davies step for a moment from the aircraft, to return rubbing his hands and blowing on his fingers. The plane, heated by the running of the engines, began to cool off. The conference went on and on, those on the spot putting the P.M. and Foreign Secretary wise to the latest moves.

About 4 o'clock I was called in. Frankly I felt terrified. Mr. Churchill, wrapped up in overcoat and scarf, looked flushed and uneasy, and remembering the illness which had stricken him two or three times previously, I wondered what on earth we should do in this witheringly cold place under the fire of rebel forces, if he were again to contract a feverish cold—which at that moment looked not unlikely. My anxiety increased when I saw the Inspector's red nose and cheeks, and poor Sawyers, who had had no time for lunch, looking half dead. This was no place for anyone to be taken ill, and where in this embattled city was to be found a warm and comfortable resting-place for the Prime Minister?

He dictated a Press communiqué. The table was sloping, the light was bad; the wind howled, and jerked the aircraft up and down; once he stopped and said, "That was cannon-fire"; with cold hands it was hard to type, and there was no klop handy. However, it was managed, and when the communiqué had been hacked about and retyped ready for issue, it was finally decided that the party would be housed aboard H.M.S. *Ajax,* a cruiser, Flagship of the Eastern Mediterranean fleet, now standing by in the Piraeus harbour. The British Embassy had been considered, but judged ill-suited for visitors: it had been for some days under siege, without light and with very little food, though things were now improving.

Thereafter the Prime Minister and others drove off in an armoured van. There was some delay while we unloaded, and shortly after 5 a.m. we, too, left the airfield.

I cannot resist here describing the odd situation in which Marian, Sawyers and I then found ourselves. The wind blew like the end of the world. The airfield was bleak and unfriendly, with piled-up snow and masses of tumbleweed rolling about. We were hustled, with no time for thought or anxiety, into a second armoured van by some poor soldiers who had been waiting around for two hours or so and looked half frozen. We were cold and hungry, Marian had a rotten cough and Sawyers was just starting a cold. We sat in swivel chairs fitted on to the iron floor, piled around with luggage and our secret boxes, Mr. Churchill's coat over our knees, and every time the van swung round a corner or crashed over a bump, boxes and bags fell on to our heads. Suddenly something snapped, and we began to laugh. We laughed and laughed and laughed, till Marian and Sawyers were convulsed with coughing, at which we all laughed more than ever. The van bumped and jarred through the Athens streets for forty-five minutes, till we reached the Naval College, where we were disembarked by some poor frozen Naval officers who had also been waiting several hours.

But what a strange place we had come to! It was a deserted rocky shore. And there was the Piraeus, the harbour of Athens. Far out, and away to right and left, some lights were twinkling. The moon was almost full and great stars hung in the sky. We were asked to keep silent; one never knew who was about. Clutching secret boxes under both arms and helped by the officers, we scrambled down some rocks and over a few strands of barbed wire, then to some steep steps, little more than a ladder. Someone said, "Take care—the top step is broken," and so with great caution we descended to a small jetty, where a motor-launch was waiting to take us to *Ajax*.

It was a relief to be somewhere at last, to be crossing that beautiful bay in the moonlight, a stiffish breeze freshening us.

Aboard *Ajax* a conference was already in progress with the Greek Prime Minister and Archbishop Damaskinos. A quaint incident had occurred. There is a custom in the Royal Navy that on Christmas Day fancy dress may be worn by naval ratings, and the Archbishop had been much disconcerted on arrival to be greeted with cheers and laughter from some of the ship's company, who imagined him to be one of themselves dressed up. He was indeed a majestic figure in his long black cassock and high black "chef's" hat, wearing an immense white beard, glasses and a silver ikon hanging low around his neck.

As usual, officers were turned out of their cabins to accommodate us. They explained that this was more difficult than it might have been at another time, as the Admiral had recently arrived aboard with his personal staff, and doubling up had already taken place.

The next three days were very exciting for Marian and me. We were much spoiled by all aboard. We worked hard, for both the Prime Minister and the Foreign Secretary, and I think earned our passage. We felt the entire company of *Ajax* were our oldest friends.

The harbour was a beautiful sight—brilliant blue water, stirred most of the time by a stiff breeze, low mountains all around, some on the mainland and some on the surrounding islands, blue in the evening and black at night. The sunrises and sunsets were brilliant, and about sundown a strange bright light seemed to come over the cream-coloured buildings which covered the shore in front of us. There on a hill high above Athens could be seen the Acropolis.

The morning after our arrival the ship was straddled by shells, though none landed too close for safety. After the air raids it seemed very little. Later in the day *Ajax* was moved farther out into the harbour. The sound of cannon-fire was frequent, and one could see Beaufighters strafing—diving and firing rockets. In the afternoon a big conference was held at the Embassy—the Prime Minister and Foreign Secretary met the leaders of the Greek Government, together with the E.L.A.S. Communist leaders, in an attempt to bring about a settlement. One of us had to go to report the meeting, so we tossed and Marian won. That was her big day, and it must have been intensely interesting. The E.L.A.S. spokesmen looked no better than brigands, and at first appeared mightily suspicious; later in the afternoon, Mr. Churchill and Mr. Eden withdrew, and discussions were held between Greek and Greek alone.

The next morning Mr. Churchill again went ashore, and outside the Embassy was shot at and missed. A woman was hit, and died there in front of the party. Within the Embassy, talks proceeded and arrangements were made for a Press Conference to be held there in the afternoon.

Meanwhile, aboard *Ajax* Marian and I had been invited by the Admiral to lunch with him and the Captain. Just as the meal was ending a naval rating entered, snapped to attention, and handed over an Emergency Signal, which the Captain opened. Miss Layton was to report at the Embassy with all possible speed. Heavens, that's *me!*—where's my hat, coat—case of stationery?

I was piped overboard, the Captain and others saluting, and rushed to the crazy pier in the Admiral's barge, where a scout car was waiting. I hopped in beside an Army Captain, and we tore through the streets of Athens. Three times we drew up, reversed and chose another route, as he spied trouble ahead. We drove quite near the Acropolis.

The Press Conference, which I was to report, was attended by about thirty correspondents, Britishers, Americans, pro-and anti-E.L.A.S. Greeks, and so on. The Prime Minister sat in his overcoat, backed by Messrs. Eden, Alexander, Macmillan, Leeper and Scobie, and spoke very fast. Frequently he was interrupted by the booming of guns, and once there was such a prolonged roll that I lost what he said, though I sat behind with my ear almost on his shoulder. Questions were then allowed, and he replied. This lasted in all about an hour, and I wrote about 4,000 words.

This had then to be typed at top speed. I retired to the cellar, where the staff were working for the sake of warmth and safety, and read out my outlines to one of the Embassy staff, who typed like the wind.

Halfway through, Mr. Colville came in to tell me, "Go to the Prime Minister—he wants to dictate." I went up into the cold, lamp-lit room. Mr. Churchill was sitting in one corner in an armchair, wearing his coat and with a rug over his knees. Near him sat the mighty figure of Archbishop Damaskinos in his impressive attire, stately and dignified, an interpreter looming behind. There was complete silence as I walked in, book in hand, and as I sat down near the Prime Minister I felt my knees nearly give in under me. Not personal fright—the air just seemed heavy with something awe-inspiring. Mr. Churchill dictated a letter to the E.L.A.S. Communist leaders, the Archbishop interpolating a few sentences through the interpreter, and I went hastily off to type it out. Perhaps I cannot quite make the reader understand the deep impression of that scene. We were, after all, in the middle of a shooting war.

When the report of the Press Conference was done, the P.M. hacked it about and a Press statement was issued. About 7 o'clock we left the Embassy. I got into the second armoured van and found myself seated between Mr. Eden, in beautiful Homburg hat, and Field-Marshal Alexander, in maroon beret. They were moderately chatty. Once or twice as we bumped and clattered through the streets I heard the sound of gunfire, and could not help reflecting how surprised my mother would be if she could have a sudden bird's-eye view of where I was sitting.

We reached the jetty, had the usual struggle down the broken steps, and boarded the Admiral's barge. This is not, of course, a barge in the usual sense, but a very super speedboat with a small cabin to seat about four. Mr. Churchill was already inside, and he told me to come in and share the rug he had over his knees. So I sat beside him, while Hero No. 2, the Field-Marshal, sat Opposite and looked with a grin at W. Churchill and E. Layton sharing a fur rug. Small fry such as Mr. Macmillan and Mr. Leeper stood outside, blown by the wind and wet with salty spray.

I hope the reader will not be misled into thinking my head was expanding!

That night Marian and I both worked flat out until 2.30, too excited to feel tired. We collected one souvenir each; someone had given us some Greek banknotes, and we each got Mr. Churchill, Mr. Eden and Field-Marshal Alexander to put their signature on one for us, my only effort in autograph hunting in all those years.

Next afternoon, after heartfelt good-byes, we left. Soon we were circling high above the Piraeus in our beautiful bird; looking down, we could see *Ajax* in the blue water.

The author at her desk at Chequers.

The author and Marion with officers aboard H.M.S. *Ajax*.

17

I do not know whether perhaps Marian and I were a little self-assured when we got back home. We were certainly the objects of much interest. We had been on duty under gunfire and shellfire—if you stretched the point a little. We had almost been In Danger. We had dashed to Athens—*Athens*—for Christmas; fancy that!

It seemed only a short time after this adventure before we were once again on the move, this time to Malta and Yalta. There was to be a meeting of Prime Minister and President at Malta preliminary to the Big Three meeting at Yalta, in the Crimea.

Early one morning at the end of January Marian and I, in company with various Foreign Office officials, took off in a Liberator, Mediterranean-bound. We were to arrive some hours earlier than the Prime Minister, Private Secretaries, Commander Thompson and Peter, who were coming in the Skymaster, and were to prepare the office aboard the cruiser H.M.S. *Orion* in Grand Harbour, which was to be our temporary hotel. Unfortunately, the Liberator's heating apparatus was not functioning, and before Malta was reached we became nearly frozen, blobs of ice jingling round our chins from our breath and the temperature in the plane below zero, we were told. Fortunately, I can ascribe partly to our chilled state the following rather discreditable incident.

On arrival at Luqa airfield, we tumbled half-frozen from the aircraft, to be welcomed by a waiting crowd of Service personnel. One officer, whose face seemed familiar, singled out Marian and me, saying: "Come along, you two, I'll take you to the harbour in my car." As we walked away with him, Marian said, "Oh yes, you're Bill, aren't you?"—whereat he drew himself up rather stiffly and said, "Straight's the name." "Marian," I whispered urgently, "Air-Commodore Whitney Straight." We had last seen him at Cairo West airfield. Presently I said, by way of easing matters, "Have you been transferred here?" He answered, stiffer than before, "Oh, this is another of my stations." Too late I registered that he was Air Officer Commanding Mediterranean Theatre.

When we were alone we were convulsed with giggles. Were we really becoming so blasé that we could insult Commanders-in-Chief right, left and centre?

We hurried aboard H.M.S. *Orion* and were received by the Commander, who didn't seem too much impressed—in fact, he seemed not even to have heard of us or our exploits. Strange. We asked for our office, but he knew nothing of the prospect. We asked to see the Captain, who soon arrived—he was a tall, horse-faced man—and we asked with much politeness where we might set up office. But he seemed to have heard nothing of the necessity either, and he was considerably alarmed at the possibility that we might have to stay aboard; females—impossible! "But really," we said, "we often stay aboard naval ships. Now please let us have some place where we can set up office; the Prime Minister will be here any time now." At last we were reluctantly given the Admiral's office, as no Admiral was in residence, and as soon as Mr. Churchill came aboard he walked in to see if everything was prepared for him. We hoped the Captain realized the mistake he had nearly made.

The Foreign Secretary and his staff were quartered in H.M.S. *Sirius* opposite us in French Creek. There was first a conference of the British and American staffs, and after about three days the President arrived in the U.S. cruiser *Quincy*. It was a memorable sight. Every man-jack aboard *Orion* and *Sirius* was drawn up to attention: the P.M., wearing reefer jacket and yachting cap, was ready on *Orion's* quarter-deck. The morning sun was bright, and the buildings pushed up their shattered and sharply white outlines into a clear sky. At last the *Quincy* was seen entering Grand Harbour, passing the entrance to French Creek and then backing slowly into it, to tie up just ahead of *Orion*. Royal Marine bands played the Stars and Stripes; bells rang; hooters sounded; every soldier stood to attention. The Prime Minister stood a little ahead of the saluting officers, and saluted the President, who, clad in tweeds, sat in his chair on the gun-deck and saluted in return.

We had heard that the President had been ill, but were not prepared for the change there was in him. He looked much aged. This was even more apparent at closer quarters; he appeared frail and haggard.

The Prime Minister went at once aboard *Quincy,* and they spent the rest of the day together.

While these events were taking place, we had news of a tragic nature. One of our transport aircraft, carrying staff to Yalta, had "ditched" in the sea near Lampedusa, and of the six crew and thirteen passengers only five crew had survived, having been thrown from the nose of the aircraft. We had all known the Conference personnel, had been on several trips with them, and we felt heavy-hearted.

That night we said good-bye to *Orion*. Before we left, the Prime Minister visited the wardroom, where Marian and I were waiting with our new-found friends. In thanking the assembled officers, he said, "I hope you've taken good care of my Young Ladies. They travel everywhere with me"—and we followed him off to a heart-warming rendering of "Good night, Ladies".

We took off from Luqa in a York aircraft, in company with fourteen other young women from the various offices, lying in rows on the floor of the plane. I think we all felt uncertain after the bad news of the day, but by 8 a.m. the following morning we had reached our destination.

We came down at Saki airfield, near Simferopol, where I was warmly welcomed by my old pal General Yermetchenko. From there we were driven for five hours along the coast to Yalta, which in the olden days had been *the* Black Sea resort for the wealthy. It was picturesque country, dark-green cypresses and terracotta earth. We passed some magnificent country villas, now looking shattered and uncared for, and came at last to the Vorontsov Villa, where the British delegation was to be housed.

This had been built in 1837 by one Prince Vorontsov as his summer residence, at a cost of three million roubles. It stood in a pleasant park surrounded by cypress and olive trees, and it looked like a Grimm's fairy-story castle. One side reminded one of an ancient British keep—round, castellated towers and ivy-covered walls; the other looked something like a vast Taj Mahal. From an impressive archway facing the Black Sea, high, pointed and mosaic-ed, one walked down steps flanked by six white stone lions—two couchant, two rising and two standing.

Within were accommodated the Prime Minister, the Foreign Secretary, Field-Marshals Alexander and Maitland-Wilson, the three Chiefs of Staff, General Ismay, and various others, and a few of the staffs who accompanied them. I was lucky to be included, and shared a bedroom with my opposite number from the Foreign Office. Marian and I were now joined by Jo, who had flown direct from London, and the two of them, together with the greater part of the staffs, were put up in a building a mile or so off, entailing much hurrying to and fro in cars.

The Vorontsov Villa boasted several banqueting halls, various reception rooms, a conservatory containing lemon trees and many ferns, and so on; but washing facilities seemed to have been neglected. It appeared that Prince and Princess Vorontsov had concentrated more on eating than on bathing. One bath and three small washbasins served this enormous Palace, and in the morning one queued with impatient Generals and embarrassed Admirals, all carrying their shaving kit and wishing that their dressing-gowns had been long enough to cover their bare ankles.

Despite these glamorous surroundings, this was the least enjoyable of the Conferences I attended. Naturally, not from the point of view of entertainment; that did not enter. There seemed to be an air of dissatisfaction and disquiet. Instead of our usual happy flap, there was hardly enough for us to do. The Prime Minister was restless and little inclined for work. We almost longed for the time to come to an end. Peter and I went for several walks in the hills around the Palace, and saw a little of the simple Russian people living there. They seemed very friendly and un-Communist, as one thinks of Communists.

One night, towards the end of our stay, the Prime Minister invited the President and Marshal Stalin and the three Foreign Secretaries to dine at the Vorontsov Palace. We were all allowed to gather in the hall to watch the arrival. Mr. Churchill was looking his best in khaki uniform with three rows of ribbons. His two detectives were at hand, but not greatly in evidence. Presently there was a stir at the doorway and the President was wheeled in, surrounded by a posse of behatted and bulldog-jawed Secret Service men, whose dark looks of suspicion were like Hawkshaw's best. The Prime Minister greeted him, and he was taken into the reception room. Then a greater stir took place as Marshal Stalin arrived, accompanied by about twenty Soviet Guards, who pressed roughly in behind and around him. I was standing alongside the door of entry. He handed his red-banded cap to a Guard, took off his Army greatcoat and for a moment was just about to hang it on me, thinking, as he saw me out of the corner of his eye, that I was the coatstand—then pulled himself up and placed it upon the proper hook. Later, we ourselves invited about six of the President's Secret Service men to dinner. It was one of the funniest evenings on record. By this time we felt we knew some of them quite well. They seemed to talk in the way I had previously associated only with Damon Runyon's books—"Chee, dis sure is swell", etc. Fortunately we managed to get Sawyers on the go, and he entertained the company with reports of our various trips, the different beds in which Mr. Churchill had slept, and so on. For instance, the one at Marrakesh had been, according to him, only six inches off the floor. Perhaps what Sawyers said was never so funny, but his mannerisms, giggle, lisp and rolling eyes made him at times what one might call "a perfect scream". Our gallants enjoyed the evening to the full, at times slapping their sides and "hollering" with raucous laughter, and we were invited to visit their favourite nightclubs with them on our next trip to Washington.

Shortly after this evening Mr. Churchill bade farewell to his great friend Franklin D. Roosevelt. They did not meet again.

On the way home we spent three days at Cairo, after which we were to fly back to London. It so happened that this time for convenience of transport I was to travel in the P.M.'s own Skymaster, along with the Private Secretaries, Commander Thompson, Peter Kinna, a Detective-Inspector and Sawyers. We were due to take off at 2 a.m., and about 1 o'clock we all went aboard. Mr. Churchill was in one of his teasing moods, and as we all waited in the saloon of the aircraft he kept up an amusing conversation with the Private Secretaries and Commander Thompson, which made us all laugh. Presently he looked round to where Peter (never a large man) was sitting, and said, "Mr. Kinna, do you remember one time when we were leaving Tripoli, and I said that if we came down in the desert you wouldn't be much good as a meal?—well, the same applies now." Then his eye travelled on to me. "However," he continued, "we shall be all right this time as we have Miss Layton, and she will keep us going for at least ten days." There were subdued giggles all round. Then the Flight Engineer appeared and asked that two persons go forward for the take-off, to correct the aircraft's balance. Mr. Churchill broke into the arrangements—"No, no, don't send Mr. Kinna, he's no good; Miss Layton must act as ballast" (more giggles)—and so the detective and I went to the nose.

I was very glad to be given the opportunity. The crew had been our firm friends for some time, but I had never actually seen them in operation. We taxied to the end of the flare path, then Bill, the Captain, revved up the engines and went over the instruments to see everything was in order. He looked serious; no doubt he was feeling the responsibility of the precious life whose safety was in his hands. He went over the instruments a second time, then we started up the flare path, the lights flashing past—gathered strength and roared off into the sky. Bill seemed calm and full of confidence, but afterwards he told me, "I'm always terrified inside at take-off and landing."

In the morning I went aft to the Prime Minister's cabin in case he wanted to dictate. I perched on the typewriter box, which Sawyers brought in, and tried not to fall off when the plane jerked, which it frequently did. He lay against his pillows exactly as he did at home, his Box beside him, and every now and then his cigar would go out and he would want the ashtray and matches, or his pencil would roll to the floor and have to be retrieved. Sometimes he would look from the window and say, "Oh, now we're crossing the coast of France", or "What is that river? Go and ask the Captain, and find out what height we're flying at." I wrote, or popped in and out, or just sat and waited, exactly as we always did at the Annexe—and yet I was in the tail of an aircraft with the greatest man in the world, at a cardinal moment in history, flying 6,000 feet above the Mediterranean and France, while he carried on the work of the British Government. Extraordinary. Unbelievable, really.

The author in 1958 with her husband, Frans, François 2, Deborah 7, Andrea 11.

Elizabeth Nel 123

Mr. Churchill at the end of his V.E. broadcast.

18

The war in Europe was drawing to its end. With the danger to our country and our cause receding, it was only natural that our thoughts should begin turning to our own lives and prospects. In the office we were all tired. Mrs. Hill looked far from robust. Personally I had begun to feel it essential to make a change. I found it difficult to sleep even for the short time we had in bed. I longed as never before for peace to come, and knew that if it had not been in sight I could never have kept up the pace, but must have fallen by the wayside, as had various colleagues before me. I determined that as soon as convenient after the war I would go home to my own country of Canada: hard as it would be to leave Mr. Churchill's service, I knew there were countless others who would willingly step into my shoes.

The British nation was tired. Rockets and flying-bombs still came daily, perhaps almost hourly, and there were many, particularly in the eastern parts of London, who were nearly at breaking-point. But, of course, the knowledge that the struggle was nearly over kept everyone going.

Halfway through March Mrs. Churchill, accompanied by Ham, set out on a tour of Russian hospitals. She had inspired and led the Red Cross "Aid to Russia" fund, and had put an enormous amount of time and work into the scheme, and now she was invited to tour the hospitals which had benefited from her efforts. She was to be gone about two months.

With her went any restraint on the P.M.'s peculiar ideas of time. Our unusual working hours became fantastic. No one could induce Mr. Churchill to go to bed before 3.30 or 4 a.m. His afternoon rest would sometimes only be started at 8 p.m., dinner would be at 9.30 or later, and when there had been "business" visitors to dine, the evening's work might only start at 1.30.

Mr. Lloyd George died, and next day Mr. Churchill paid a most eloquent tribute to him in the House of Commons. That was conceived and dictated in the early hours of the morning preceding its delivery, and put into Speech Form as the darkness ebbed.

In those days there were few statements and broadcasts to be given; it seemed that everything was waiting for the end of the war. There was something on Mr. Churchill's mind—had been ever since Yalta. He would sit talking, talking through the evening with his close friends and advisers. Sometimes one would wait up for him till 3.30, but there would be no dictation. Some evenings one would sit in the room while he worked and talked.

One did not have to think very hard to know what it was that was troubling him. It was the deterioration in the relations between ourselves and the Soviet Union.

There was one evening I remember well. Mr. Churchill sat in his study with several colleagues—Mr. Brendan Bracken, then Minister of Information, Lord Beaverbrook, who was Lord Privy Seal, and Mr. James Stuart, the Chief Whip—discussing post-war plans, or perhaps they were listening to the P.M.'s post-war plans. The Private Secretary (it was Mr. Peck) and I waited patiently for some sign of Duty or of Bed to appear. The hours passed slowly—2 o'clock, 3 o'clock—and presently we could bear it no longer. Mr. Peck decided we had better try to remind the Prime Minister of the time. He piled some official boxes on the edge of the table, then jarred the bottom one so that they all fell on the floor. There was a terrible crash; we smothered our giggles and waited, but nothing happened, though sometimes if one coughed in the office, the buzzer would sound and one would be told "Too much noise".

Some time later Mr. Peck decided to have another go.

"Now," he said, "I'll show you what happened when I was on duty the other morning." He balanced the iron fire-shovel on the iron fireguard with the end under the lip of the scuttle, where he said it had been put by the charwoman. Then he sat at his desk near the fireplace and said, "Now, when the buzzer went ...", got up and rushed for the door, knocking the shovel into the fireplace with the most frightful clatter imaginable. I had to retire from the room to have my laugh out. But still nothing happened. At 4 o'clock we just didn't care any longer. Mr. Peck took the shovel as a bat and I threw at him anything I could reach, so that rubbers, balls of paper and small lumps of coal went flying round the room. At last Mr. Stuart emerged from the study, shaking with laughter. He told us that when the worst crash came he laughed, and the P.M., who was much engrossed in his subject, said sternly, "It's all very well for you to laugh, you haven't got any tubercular children." It was 4.30 when Bed was finally announced.

And then something tragic happened. In April President Roosevelt died. We had the news about midnight, and some minutes later I was hurried into the study for dictation. Mr. Churchill was sitting crumpled up in his chair, his face white. When he dictated he was gentle as a lamb, but his voice sounded quite dead.

The next day he paid tribute in the House to Mr. Roosevelt. As we sat hastily putting his words into Speech Form, we could hear over the kitchen staff's radio a memorial service from St. Paul's Cathedral. The boys' choir sang in their high, clear voices the Battle Hymn of the American Republic, which tune I had previously imagined belonged exclusively to "John Brown's Body". It was slow and beautiful, and made one want to cry.

There was a feeling of relief when the first telegrams from Mr. Truman arrived. Obviously he intended to maintain the spirit of friendship and co-operation, and he seemed to know what he was talking about.

At about this time we had the worst weekend on record. First we were due to leave for Chequers as usual on the Friday afternoon. When the rest of the cavalcade had departed, leaving only the Prime Minister, Mr. Rowan, Commander Thompson and me in London, Mr. Churchill decided to stay until after dinner. The hours dragged by, then about 11.30 we heard that we were to remain in town for the night. No Sawyers—and Mrs. Landemare already away for the weekend. But we managed—I stayed up till 4 o'clock and was on duty again by 8.30.

For the rest of the weekend, which was spent at Chequers, we lived in a whirl. Dr. Gerbrandy, the Netherlands Prime Minister, a kindly little man with white hair and moustaches, called upon Mr. Churchill in a terrible state of anxiety. Secret reports had reached him that Seyss Inquart, the Nazi ruler of Holland, intended cutting the dykes and flooding precious land reclaimed over hundreds of years, unless the advance of the Allied armies was arrested. Top Secret, Most Urgent papers flashed to and fro, but there was nothing that could be done; our liberating armies *had* to go on. Then reports began to come in of the finding of the "atrocity" camps. Everything hummed, typewriters, telephone wires and jangled nerves, and night was turned into day. It was one of our top-line flaps.

April passed and May came. Victory was upon us. One morning at Chequers a telegram came over the Scrambler from Field-Marshal Alexander to say that the first overtures for an armistice in his sector of the front had reached him.

I was on early duty, and having typed this out in great excitement, rushed up to Mr. Churchill's room to give it to him. However, my enthusiasm was misplaced. He was in a bad humour, presumably the result of too little sleep. He avoided my eye, and displayed not the slightest interest in the news, as if wars ended every day. But later on he was hanging anxiously about the office for the telephone to ring, taking the telegrams direct to his ear instead of *via* our shorthand books. That evening he was as thrilled as any boy with the exciting news.

Rather ashamedly I preserved a nearly whole cigar that he lit up and forgot to finish, and though not as a rule a souvenir collector, I have it to this day.

Soon all the Germans in Italy and the Southern Redoubt of Austria had surrendered unconditionally. Then we heard that Admiral-General von Friedeburg, Commander-in-Chief of the German Navy, was negotiating in the west with Field-Marshal Montgomery, and in a day or so all the Germans in Holland, Denmark and Schleswig-Holstein had surrendered.

This was all very exciting and rewarding. I feel I should here quote a piece from my diary, an account of my own duties in the middle of these epic happenings, and this must have been the 4th May:

"Friday was one of the silliest days I've ever known. When one has had the night off and is on early duty, one arises (at home) at 7, leaves the flat at 7.30, arrives at work at 8.03, has breakfast (provided by Mrs. Landemare) in the office and is all ready, teeth cleaned and shoes shining, at 8.30. Often as not nowadays HE doesn't wake up till 10 or so, and then sometimes he has to get up for an 11 o'clock meeting or something, which means he just reads the morning papers and does no work before arising. On these occasions one feels one might just as well be at the bottom of the ocean, and the morning is entirely wasted. That is what happened to me on Friday. Then all afternoon from 2 till 7.30 I was busily engaged in disposing of portions of a monstrous cheese which had been sent to him as a gift. It really was a whopper, and about 15 chunks had to be dispersed or delivered, lists of names submitted, changes made, rechanges, etc., telephone calls, trips between No.10 and the Annexe (I think I went five times the double journey), until I could have chucked the whole blinking cheese into the river. I do hope the recipients enjoyed it, and remembered to eat it before it went bad."

I guess an occasional day of frustration doesn't harm anyone.

It so happened that Monday, 7th May, was my night on late duty. There was an atmosphere of great excitement in the office; we knew that the unconditional surrender terms had been signed. The war in Europe was not yet officially over, but everyone seemed to know that it would be by tomorrow, and as I walked round St. James's Park during the dinner hour there was a good deal of shouting, cheering and singing going on. Crowds were gathering, wearing silly paper hats and blowing whistles and waving flags—throwing confetti, playing banjos and mouth-organs, banging cymbals, whirling crackly things round and round—anything to make one feel joyous and carefree. Later that night, when I went into the study for dictation, Mr. Churchill looked up and said, "Hullo, Miss Layton …

well, the war's over, you've played your part." As the evening progressed, a terrific thunderstorm broke—flashes, bangs and crashes. Once or twice he looked up and said, with a twinkle, "What was that?—oh, only thunder," or, "Was that an explosion?" or, "Might as well have another war." It was 3.45 before he went to bed, and 4.30 by the time I had finished off the typing.

V.E. Day, 8th May, was a joyful time for us all. In the morning I went to St. Paul's Cathedral, and we sang "Praise, my soul, the King of Heaven"—meaning it. In the afternoon the Prime Minister was to make a short statement to the nation, timed for 3 o'clock. The entire staff turned up at No.10 from the Annexe for the occasion, and we all stood outside the Cabinet Room door. Just before 3 we heard a great trumpeting sound over the loudspeaker as he blew his nose, then some remarks—"Pull down that blind"—"What are you doing with that? No, leave it there"—"Move a little further away, please"—etc., but, of course, this was only coming out to us, he was not yet on the general air. After his statement, the text of which can be read elsewhere, we all rushed downstairs and out into the garden to line the path to the garden door, and when he came out to go to the House to give his statement again we clapped and clapped, and I think there were tears in his eyes as he beamed and said, "Thank you all, thank you very much."

Outside, through the Horse Guards Parade, along Birdcage Walk and Great George Street, through Parliament Square, the whole place was cram-jammed with people waiting to welcome him. They cheered and shouted "Good old Winnie", and some pressed forward to pat the car and jump on the running-board, so that it was almost impossible for it to move and it took quite thirty minutes to drive the quarter of a mile.

That night he and members of the War Cabinet appeared on a balcony overlooking Parliament Street and Square. Some of us were able to squeeze on to a small part adjoining, to watch the fun. Flags and bunting had been put up, and floodlights were directed upon the balcony. A crowd which some estimated at 20,000 stood below—the roar of their cheering seeming almost to lift one off one's feet. It was just a sea of faces and waving arms. As Mr. Churchill emerged, the noise increased almost to deafening point. Microphones were ready. He knew so well what to say. He congratulated the Londoners on their fortitude, saying, "I always said 'London can take it.' Were we downhearted?" … The response was overwhelming. He mentioned Japan, and the crowd booed happily. Then he began the first few words of "Land of Hope and Glory", and the multitude took it up with a will.

I shall always remember Mr. Churchill as he was at that moment—spick-and-span in black coat and striped trousers, a flower in his buttonhole, his face smooth and pink, a man medium in height and somewhat round of figure, a man whose character contained all the elements of greatness and whose knowledge of human nature made him understand equally the reactions of his valet and of Heads of other States.

That was Mr. Churchill's hour. Whatever was to come, nothing could take it from him. The entire nation came forward to show its gratitude and affection for the man whose courage had been an inspiration in its darkest hours. For the next few days he could not move from the office without being mobbed in every street. He took to driving in an open car, so that he could sit on the back and wave his hat to the crowds, who appeared from nowhere wherever he was to be seen. Letters, telegrams and gifts poured into the office from all over the country.

I think he enjoyed every minute of it. He knew he deserved it. I expect that, being the old Parliamentarian he is, he knew it could not last. Already his thoughts were fully enmeshed in the trials that lay ahead; winning the peace might prove more difficult than winning the war. Already our relations with the Soviet had changed; little by little, in the months since Yalta, the comradeliness of our wartime association seemed to have vanished. The question of Poland's frontiers was a stumbling-block. There was no longer mutual confidence and exchange of ideas. "How are we to work together," said Mr. Churchill, "if an iron curtain is to be drawn down between us, and only occasionally raised to allow a face, and not a very pleasant face at that, to peer through at us?"

So that although Victory in Europe was a time for unstinted rejoicing, one felt that a shadow lay ahead. But I don't think one of us ever seriously imagined that Winston Churchill would not be there to lead the nation through its post-war trials.

19

And now a new phase began. The Coalition Government was dissolved, and a Conservative Caretaker Government was formed until such time as the elections had decided whom the country wanted to rule her. Electioneering started in a big way.

I found this far less to my taste than struggling along to win the war. In the office Mrs. Hill and I were now to the fore: the others, including the Private Secretaries, being Civil Servants, could not take part in electioneering.

During June the campaign was at its height. Mr. Churchill made four broadcasts, all of them fairly lengthy, and did a considerable amount of touring about the country speaking on behalf of Conservative candidates. First, there was his own constituency of Woodford in Essex, where he was to be opposed by some hopeful farmer. Here he had a rapturous welcome, despite the drizzling rain; he stopped to speak at every hamlet, Mrs. Churchill holding an umbrella over his head, and everywhere crowds had gathered. Another day on our way to Chequers we diverted to visit Uxbridge, Beaconsfield and Aylesbury, where the entire populations seemed to have turned out. At Beaconsfield Mr. Churchill mounted to the balcony of the Red Lion Inn, from which Disraeli spoke at election time, and addressed a vast crowd.

Then there was a tremendous cross-country tour lasting about five days. I went on this occasion, as Mrs. Hill was otherwise engaged. The first day we drove through to the Midlands—Buckingham, Towcester, Rugby, Leamington, Warwick, Coventry and Birmingham. Wherever we went, dense crowds had turned out to see and cheer Mr. Churchill, who was in an open car. Sarah drove with her father, and Commander Thompson and I preceded them in the loudspeaker car; we could see the smiles that lit up all faces as they caught sight of him, and hear the continual repetition of "There he is, there he is" from those lining the route. We stopped about fifteen times during the day, and Mr. Churchill spoke on behalf of his candidates.

We stayed the night aboard our train, and the following day "did" Leeds, Halifax, Bradford, Preston and so forth, receiving the same welcome. Then on to Glasgow and Edinburgh, and here I was involved in a rather amusing incident.

Driving through the country in the open car had slightly inflamed Mr. Churchill's eyes. On this day he left the train at a siding just outside Glasgow about 12.30, for a tour of the city. This was to be followed by an official luncheon at the Conservative Club at 1.30, after which the Prime Minister was to travel by road to Edinburgh. I was told to hurry into the shopping centre by tram, purchase some special eye lotion (the prescription for which I had obtained by telephone from Lord Moran in London), deliver this to the Club and return to the train, which was due to leave for Edinburgh at 2 o'clock.

I did as instructed, telling the train officials that I would surely be back by 2 o'clock. But the tram was slow, and the prescription, when I found a chemist who could produce the right materials, took nearly an *hour* to be made up; and it was 1.50 by the time I arrived, hurried and anxious, outside the Club in a taxi.

I noticed the streets, which were heavily lined with people, seemed very neat and well-controlled and expectant, but thought, "They must be waiting for him to come out after lunch." At the front entrance a wave of horrified commissionaires and attendants ordered me to move on, but despite their vigorous protests I elbowed my way into the Club and demanded to see Sawyers. Just at that moment there were roars and cheers, and the party arrived, having lost thirty minutes *en route*. Someone thrust me hastily behind a curtain—just in time, as the gold-braided reception committee swept forward to welcome the important visitors.

Catching the eye of Inspector Hughes, the detective, I delivered my precious parcel. Alas, it was now almost 2 o'clock, and if the train left without me, what should I do?—how should I get to Edinburgh?—what would Mr. Churchill say if no one was there to take down the news from London? I rushed to a telephone, and tried in vain to contact the small siding, which was at least half an hour's ride by tram from where I was.

A few minutes later, as I stood in the hall of the Club wondering what to do, nearly in tears, I was approached by a large and kindly officer in police uniform, with silver leaves around his cap and a goodly array of silver on his chest. He asked what was the matter, and when I told him he said: "Don't you worry, I am the Chief Constable of Glasgow, and I'll see you get there." So he and his second-in-command escorted me from the Club in lordly fashion, and into a huge car with a flag streaming from the front. Seated between my two Good Samaritans, I was driven with all possible speed through back streets and topsy-turvy places to the siding, where we found the train steamed up and the officials anxiously looking at their watches. They could not have been more polite when they saw who was rolling up.

Soon we were back in London. Little did we guess that this wonderful reception of Mr. Churchill was an expression of thanks for the past rather than an indication of the future. I think it was misleading. Knowing nothing of British elections, I once or twice asked the Private Secretaries what they thought the outcome would be. The answer was, "Probably a reduced majority; however, with elections you never can tell." All the same, I don't think the possibility of defeat was seriously considered in the office.

I had another electioneering adventure. One evening Mr. Churchill was to speak at a huge open-air meeting in the Walthamstow Stadium, about forty-five minutes' drive from Whitehall. He left at 6 o'clock. We watched him away, then returned to the flat, where to our horror we found he had left his speech notes behind. I collared a car and a good driver, and simply flew after him, hatless and coatless. Of course, we couldn't catch him. When we reached the Stadium, a football ground surrounded by stands and buildings, I leapt out and battled my way through the crowd to the front entrance, where I managed to get inside. Heavens, what a huge place, and what an enormous crowd; miles and miles away in the middle of the green grass was the stand from which he would speak, but I could see he was not there yet.

All London seemed to have congregated. I took a chance on direction, and frantically pushed my way through a crowded alleyway for what seemed a mile, muttering, "Excuse me, pardon me, must get through" the whole way, till I reached a corridor along which I fancied he would walk to the stand. I dodged under a rope and through a row of pompous-looking officials; one grabbed my arm, but I shook him off, pelted to a man in uniform who was standing by an inner door, and gasped, "Oh, *do* take me to the Prime Minister, I've got his speech notes." I suppose my appearance convinced him, for he escorted me swiftly to a room within, which Mr. Churchill was about to leave, having had a few preliminary words with the Party officials. He smiled when he saw my scarlet face, took his notes, saying, "Poor lamb, have you run all the way behind the car?" and went off to his meeting. That evening I was much teased at the office.

But on that occasion Mr. Churchill had more heckling than usual, and a day or two later, when he was touring South London, a Labour stronghold, someone threw a stone and hit him. It hurt, I'm sure, not actually but inside. It was not the kind of thing one would have expected from political opponents; the British are not normally stone-throwers. It betokened feelings of which one had previously known nothing.

On the 5th July Britain voted, but the poll was to remain sealed until the 27th of that month, in order that the votes of the Forces overseas might be counted in the total.

The Potsdam Conference took place in the latter half of July. I asked to be left at home on this occasion, as I shall explain. Mr. Churchill, Mrs. Hill and others from the office went off to it, and there was a pause in the middle while the Prime Minister returned to England to be present for the declaration of the poll.

I was on duty the morning of that fateful 27th. Mr. Churchill seemed much as usual when I went in at 8.30, though he said he had not slept well. Of that horrible day I do not like to think. From unsuspecting confidence we turned to mere hope, from hope to doubt, and from doubt to the certainty of failure. At 10 o'clock the first result came in, from Salford, Manchester, where the Labour candidate had won, and from then on the figures advanced, the Map Room boys coming every few minutes with fresh results. At 25 Labour there were 7 Conservatives in, at 75 Labour 26 Conservatives, at 110 Labour 44 Conservatives, and so on. By midday we knew for sure that the landslide had taken place, with over 300 Labour victories; they were in and we were out. Even Mr. Churchill's independent-minded Opponent had polled 10,000 votes; this did not bring him near to winning the seat, but it was a cut.

The shock and sense of catastrophe were overwhelming. It seemed a lifetime since 8.30 that morning. We began to realize things we had never thought of. We no longer belonged on the Prime Minister's staff. We no longer had the official staff on which to lean. We should have to get ourselves and all our belongings out of No.10 and the Annexe, and this pretty quickly. Mrs. Hill and I were now Private Secretaries to the Leader of the Opposition.

But you will know that the little we felt for ourselves was completely lost in what we felt for Mr. Churchill. True, he was, as ever, a tower of strength and self-control. Perhaps his long life had taught him that those who hold high office are for ever open to such disappointments and can never, never make sure they will not happen. While knowing that the nation was voting out his Party rather than himself, he must still have felt the most terrible, searing hurt, intensified because of the welcome he had received on his tours of the country.

But it was more than the hurt. It was not being allowed to lead the Peace, which had been his dream while he was still leading the War. When you have worked for something day in, day out, night in, night out for five years—and held all the strings in your own hand, and seen your carefully planned schemes coming to fruition—then you cannot have that responsibility snatched away without feeling the gaping hole it leaves. It seemed particularly cruel that this should happen at this very moment, as an anti-climax to the climax, without warning, apparently without cause—and with the war against Japan still to be finished off. Roosevelt dead, Germany beaten, Churchill out—how swiftly things can change.

I shall not say much of the weeks that followed. It was a busy time. Mr. Attlee, of course, went back to Potsdam for the remainder of the Conference, taking with him the Private Secretaries, Marian and others. Within a few days we had removed from the office the visible traces of our residence there, said good-bye to Chequers and its happy associations, and bundled ourselves off. In addition to moving out, we had to cope with the greatest flood of mail ever to be received at the office, as half of the populace vented their regret and dismay that the other half should have shown such ingratitude and inflicted such a stroke upon their hero, who was indeed everyone's hero, the man who had arisen in the hour of supreme trial.

The Churchills were to buy a house at Hyde Park Gate, but in the meantime moved into the Duncan Sandys' flat in Westminster. We worked there during the week, and at the weekends we went to Chartwell. While the subject-matter contained in our Box was far less important and interesting than it had been during the last five years, Mrs. Hill and I found ourselves just as busy as before. We worked almost the same hours, but now we no longer had the office behind us. We took responsibility for all arrangements. Getting adjusted was an uncomfortable time for all—including Mr. Churchill.

Then came the dropping of the two Atom Bombs and the defeat of Japan. We were glad that V.J. came so soon after the election results, since now it could never be said that Victory in the Far East was not every bit as much *his* victory as Victory in Europe had been.

That afternoon—it was a Friday, and we were shortly to leave London for Chartwell—Mr. and Mrs. Churchill invited Mrs. Hill, Ham and me to join them in a glass of champagne, to celebrate the end of the war. We drank it to him, naturally. We could not feel the joy we had felt at V.E.

Later, driving through Westminster with Mr. Churchill, *en route* for Kent, I saw him looking out at the crowds waving flags in the street, and the bunting-draped buildings. I wondered what he was feeling; I knew it must be hurting, a bitter, bitter hurt.

Later in August Mr. Churchill decided to accept an invitation he had received from Field-Marshal Alexander to spend a holiday at Lake Como. He said he was going to do some painting, and that I should go too to look after the office side, though there would not be much work. On the 1st September we flew there, and were soon settled into a magnificent villa on the lakeshore.

20

And now comes the end of *my* story.

I had some time previously told Mr. Churchill that I intended returning to Canada when it was convenient for him to replace me. He had then kindly asked whether I would not come back after a holiday at home, but feeling I couldn't possibly live for ever within the close confines of the British way of life, I had awkwardly and ungraciously said No, I felt I must go back to Canada to stay. Now, here, on our first morning beside Lake Como I had to tell him that I had changed my plans.

I had never felt that to be a secretary was my ultimate goal, but had known that if the right man came along, be my work infinitely exciting and important, I should choose marriage. And then, just at the moment when I most needed it, when I was feeling tired and worn out with work and longing for something for myself, it happened. In May I met Lieutenant Frans Nel, a mighty South African, from Pretoria in the Transvaal, about a week after he had been released from prison camp, having been captured at Tobruk way back in 1942. There wasn't any doubt. This was it.

We had odd moments together, and I cried off from the Potsdam Conference so that we could see a little of each other—it *was* a little for there was still work to do at the office. Then he sailed away for South Africa without making any definite plan, wanting first to get home and get adjusted and find himself a job.

Then—Frans was gone, we were thrown out of office with a resounding wallop, and life was one wedge of unhappiness. I staggered along unable to collect myself and unable to sleep, longing for the time to pass and for something to happen to decide matters. It happened the night before we were to fly to Como. I arrived home at the Kensington flat after 8 o'clock—and there was a cable from Frans saying all was well, he had a job, and would I please pack up as soon as possible for South Africa. Next morning, as we took off for Italy, I was in a happy daze and nearly got left behind.

I told Mr. Churchill, and I think he was pleased. He said it was time I was married (I was then twenty-eight). The three weeks spent at Como were among the happiest I can remember, a time of rest in beautiful and peaceful surroundings with everything in life to look forward to. I had been long away from my own family, and now I should be farther off than ever; but something told me they would come and visit me before long. I had looked forward to a year or so of relaxing after the struggle and strain of the war, but now I was not to have this, for I knew that Frans and I would be starting out together from scratch. However, "a change is as good as a rest", never forget that.

We were soon back in London, my replacement was arranged, and after quite a short time I said good-bye to Winston Churchill.

I shall not try to relate my feelings on leaving him. A reader of the foregoing should be able to understand them for himself. I left feeling a different person from the one who entered, in all innocence, the whirl of haste, excitement and perpetual crisis that surrounded him. The war was over, that phase of life was ended. But even after all these years, hardly a day passes that I do not think of him.

I shall never forget the kindness with which Mr. and Mrs. Churchill bade me farewell. He was in bed with a sore throat and could only speak in a whisper; Mrs. Churchill was sitting beside him. They told me I must have four children (as they have), and said together: "One for Mother, one for Father, one for Accidents and one for Increase." After telling me a little of South Africa as he had known it, Mr. Churchill looked down the expanse of his bed and whispered hoarsely: "I know you'll keep the flag flying."

I hope he would think I have done so. A few weeks later Frans and I were married in Pretoria. Perhaps it has not been altogether easy, becoming adjusted to another country and a different way of life, where English is only one of the languages used. But I have been helped by the fact that South Africa has much in common with Canada. It was not easy to bear the children and to rear them, after the physical effort of those five years. But now that we have been blessed, most truly blessed, in the arrival of two daughters and a son, I feel that another milestone in my life has been passed. After a year in South Africa a great longing for my own family set in, but here again I was granted happiness. First my sister came from Canada, eventually to marry and settle in South Africa, and a little later my mother also migrated, to make her home alongside us.

I am truly a South African now, and a very happy one. Our children are being brought up to put South Africa first. I think they are fortunate in their dual heritage, and in good time they, like me, will be able to speak Afrikaans as fluently as English. But I remember, also, to teach them about Winston Churchill and the things he has stood for in his long lifetime. Courage. Strength. Resolution. Steadfast loyalty. Love of country. If I can only teach them these things I shall have done something, be it ever so little.

I shall never see him again. England is too far away, when you have a husband who works hard and three small children who depend on you. But I shall never forget.

Afterword

by Elizabeth Nel

It is now over 60 years since I wrote the foregoing, and it now seems appropriate that I should carry my story a little further. How time flies! It does not seem so long since Those Days.

Frans and I married in 1945—really knowing very little of each other. Different language, education, financial standing—different loyalties and occupations. We each had much to adjust to. But we had the same standards—morals, if you like—the same convictions regarding Right and Wrong, the same objectives in life—and most of all we loved each other. And so, though major adjustments were required, particularly from me, we were really very happy, and this lasted for nearly 55 years. He died in August 2000. But I have the precious children, and they never forget me, though all three live elsewhere—two in Johannesburg, the third in Cape Town. All have lovely families and all work hard to keep them. Truly, the Lord has been *so good* to me.

I have done a great deal of speaking in public about my war experience—so much so that folk may be bored to hear or read my story. But I would like to pass on some of the conclusions I have reached through the years.

People have asked: "But what did Winston Churchill actually DO, what did he achieve to reach his pinnacle?" I can tell you. I was living in London before the war, and I well remember the many pacifists who said, "We can't have another war—we haven't yet recovered from the pains and losses of the last one. Let's rather go along with Hitler, let's work with him to avoid war, he's probably not nearly as bad as portrayed. We want peace."

And what was the reaction of Winston Churchill, who knew just what Hitler had in mind? He raised a clenched fist and answered in powerful tones, "GET UP AND FIGHT!" reminding them of Britain's history, her long struggle for Freedom from invaders. His words appealed to the latent spirit of Freedom and Justice which lies deep in British hearts, and they GOT UP and they FOUGHT—by land and sea and in the air. No one can take that away from Winston Churchill. The people reacted to his courage, his determination and his absolute loyalty to Britain and all she has stood for. It was that inspiration which enabled us to win the war—not money, not clever inventions or bombs and guns. *I know—I was there* (Thump on table with fist!).

But what did I think of him as a person? Was he very difficult to work for?

Certainly he did not like having new staff, and a new face across the table was enough to put him off his work. However, provided one did not make too many mistakes, he quite soon got used to a new staff member (great relief!). All the same, entering his room for dictation, especially when it was the Cabinet Room and there were several Cabinet members present, was seen to be a serious business.

After working for some months regularly for him I realised: yes, he was difficult, yes, he was impatient, yes, he was demanding—but never impossible. Through all of this I perceived an inner kindness and appreciation. He cared—in fact, he had a loving heart, as I told many audiences, and as we all know, that conquers all. He was a dear man, as you realised when you got to know him. I still hear from his lovely daughter Mary Soames and his dear Granddaughter Celia Sandys.

There is one little story which I think does not appear in the present edition of my book—I omitted it previously thinking at the time it might cause criticism. Mr Churchill had a meeting with General de Gaulle at which the General was rough and rude. Mr Churchill was quite upset, and said within the office, "I won't see that chap again." But later Mr Churchill was ill with pneumonia, and on doctor's orders was obliged to stay at Chequers for two weeks. The General, feeling he had been rude, asked if he might come to Chequers to make peace. General Ismay and our Principal Private Secretary, Mr Martin, were present and anxious that all should go well, so they spoke out to Mr Churchill, saying for the sake of Anglo-French relations he must please forgive General de Gaulle and allow him to come. Mr Churchill, who was wearing his siren suit and well-known dragon dressing-gown, walked into the office (where I was listening to them), and said, "All right, all right, I'll be good, I'll be sweet. I'll kiss him on both cheeks—all four if you'd prefer it." How we laughed afterwards!

The fact that I am now the only one left who can tell you with absolute certainty how Winston was in the office, what he said and did, weighs rather heavily upon me—the others all being now gone, alas. So I have tried to recall relevant aspects of his leadership, which I may have omitted in the original edition of my book. He certainly said to the boys of Harrow School when he visited there in August 1941, "Never, never, Never, NEVER give in—except to conviction of Honour or Common-sense"—and I think that that was his final punch-line. I have thought of this so often, and tried to live up to it.

Elizabeth Nel 141

Elizabeth Nel at Ninety, in her home in Port Elizabeth, South Africa.

She is seen here wearing her World War II Defence Medal that was given to her by Winston Churchill.
In the background is a painting of the Drill Hall of the Prince Alfred's Guards, painted for Frans Nel, Elizabeth's husband, on his retirement.

Photograph by Lionel Heath.

Epilogue

ELIZABETH NEL TODAY
by Lionel Heath

Despite her ninety years, Elizabeth Nel greets me at the door with a warm and firm handshake accompanied by a welcoming smile and insists she be called Elizabeth. She ushers me through the sun porch into the spacious lounge/dining room of the cottage in the retirement complex where she stays. She walks without a stick but later uses one as she says she now needs a bit of security when she walks.

The cottage is tastefully decorated with furniture which falls into two main categories—good quality items bought second-hand by her and her late husband, Frans Nel, when they "had little money" and then beautifully restored and maintained, and items made by Frans himself. The walls are decorated with paintings, mainly watercolours, and various certificates awarded to her and Frans for various reasons. Some of the watercolours were painted by Frans. A number of wooden pieces of art are dotted around the room and on the wall a very realistic looking maple leaf made of metal serves as a reminder of Elizabeth's youth in Canada. The piano stands waiting for her to play "when she has a bit more time." In contrast the typewriter is out and has paper in it. She did try a computer once for a while but returned to her faithful typewriter.

Elizabeth still does all her own cooking, except for lunch on Wednesdays, but does have a lady in once a week to clean the cottage. I am impressed when, on her way to make us coffee, she nimbly bends down to pull a rug straight.

She starts talking about her two daughters, Andrea and Debbie, both of whom live in Johannesburg and her son, François, a deputy principal at a boys' primary school in Cape Town. She also speaks with pride of her seven grandchildren, but when I ask about her great grandchildren she comments that none of them is married yet and none would dare to have a child out of wedlock. Some of the younger ones are still studying.

She apologises that she has not yet had time to frame a certificate awarded to her in December 2006 at a special goodwill tea. It indicates that, after fifty years of service as a member of the Port Elizabeth branch of the National Council of Women and after many years of service to the National Executive, the title of Honorary Life Vice President of the local branch has been conferred on her. She reminisces of the days when she and her close friends, Bunty Mann, Jean van't Hoogerhuijs and Peggy Selly did Port Elizabeth proud by serving together on the national executive of the Council. She still manages to attend local meetings occasionally.

On the educational side she talks of the many interesting years she served on the school committee of the Collegiate High School for Girls where her second daughter, Debbie, was a prefect. Her commitment to the school was rewarded when she was made an honorary old girl of the school.

Her various activities did not involve any form of political organisation as her husband was a military man and they agreed that she should not become involved despite her interest. Instead she supported her husband and took an interest in things military. As a result of this she has been given honorary membership of the mess of the Prince Alfred's Guard of which Frans was officer commanding for many years and from which he retired as honorary colonel not long before his death. Under the Nationalist government an attempt was made to change the name of the guard again. It had originally changed its name from the Port Elizabeth Volunteers after a visit to South Africa by Queen Victoria's second son, Prince Alfred, and the name was too closely connected to English royalty for the government. Frans was instrumental in convincing the government that the name commemorated the visit and not the name of the visitor and the name remained. The crest and flag, however, had to be changed. Frans provided the design and Elizabeth the motto, *Fidelis et Fortis*, Faithful and Brave. The flag design and motto seem to be acceptable to the present government and today most of the members of the guard are the descendants of the nation against whom the regiment was "blooded" when the first member was killed in a battle at Umzintzani—the valley of burning bushes. The valley is near Butterworth in the Eastern Cape and gets its name from the coral trees which are covered with a mass of vivid red flowers in the late winter to early spring before the leaves emerge.

Elizabeth still attends functions in the Prince Alfred's Guard Drill Hall and says she is well received by the young men. Whenever she attends any function with a military flavour, she wears her military medal, a World War II Defence Medal. At the end of the war Churchill suggested that she and her companion should each be awarded an MBE, but his senior private secretary argued that, according to the pecking order, some other lady should be awarded one first. In reply to Churchill's retort, "Well, give her something!" the secretary gave Elizabeth and her colleague a Defence Medal each. Later thousands of these were to be awarded, but Elizabeth was the recipient of one of the first two handed out. It is still lovingly kept in cotton wool in a special box ready for the next military event.

The drill hall is also the venue where the Military History Society of the Eastern Cape meets monthly. This provides Elizabeth with another opportunity to visit the venue that means so much to her. She loves the stories told at meetings about battles of long ago, particularly those in which the Prince Alfred's guard was involved. Her appetite for historical tales is also whetted at meetings of the local Historical Society which she also attends, if possible.

Unfortunately Elizabeth is not as mobile as she was until recently. A few months ago, after bumping another car with her red Toyota, she felt she had to give up driving and now has to rely on others for lifts. Her neighbours in the complex and friends are happy to take her wherever she wishes, but she does not like to impose on them too often. In addition, her doctor has reminded her of her age and that she needs to slow down a bit and use the word, "No!" occasionally.

Elizabeth Nel has almost become a household name in certain areas of Port Elizabeth as a result of her talks on her life working for Winston Churchill. There is hardly a service or social club, school or organisation in the city and suburbs which she has not addressed at some time or other, and she has been presented with many tokens of appreciation, prominent among which is a copy of Rotary's Four Way Test, as she has been a regular speaker at Rotary meetings. She says she used to count her talks but gave up and thinks she must have given over a thousand. She says that on so many occasions she has received words and tokens of thanks, congratulations and appreciation that no more are needed.

Elizabeth was unable to end our meeting without another anecdote about Winston Churchill. This relates to a recent event and she is sure it does not appear in writing elsewhere. She refers to it as the story of "My Cigar". The event occurred at Chequers. Churchill was still in bed when a phone call came through in May 1945 from General Alexander. He told Elizabeth that the enemy in the Eastern Mediterranean had surrendered unconditionally. She typed the message and took it up to Churchill who glanced at it and threw it to one side and continued with what he was doing. She then told Mr Martin, Churchill's principal private secretary, that he had seemed not to have read the message properly. She was mistaken as he came down shortly afterwards to phone Number 10 Downing Street and spoke for a long time. Before he phoned, he lit up a cigar and had two or three puffs and then threw it into the grate. Later Elizabeth picked it up, wrapped it in cotton wool and then put it in a box. It remained in the box in one of her wardrobes for sixty years until the sixtieth anniversary of the end of the war. She contacted Phil Reed, then Curator of the Cabinet War Rooms, to offer what she called "some items of war memorabilia"—and among these was "a cigar partly smoked by Mr Churchill".[1] She had these items shipped to the Museum on 20 April 1995, on the understanding that if "they were no longer required, they should be returned to herself or her husband or, in the event they were both deceased, to her children". Also it was specifically stipulated that they should "*never be sold!*".[2] The cigar was duly given pride of place in the Churchill Museum in a display case with a spotlight shining on it. On a return visit some

---

1. Joanne Grenier-Morton, Personal Assistant to Phil Reed, the Director of the Churchill Museum and Cabinet War Rooms, has kindly offered the following additional information written by herself: "Elizabeth Nel donated 'Her Cigar' directly to the Imperial War Museum on 20 April 1995 and it has been proudly displayed at the Churchill Museum (a branch of the IWM) since its opening in 2005. I was very privileged to accompany her on her 'return visit' to the Churchill Museum in 2006. We had been incredibly lucky and honoured that she had agreed to give a lecture on her extraordinary memories at the Museum on the 7th of November 2006. She was very eager to see 'Her Cigar' again, but understandably she was very tired after the lecture that evening, so she came back especially the day after, and we spent the morning together with her daughter Andrea. I was the person she complained to that her cigar seemed to have 'shrunk'! I remember this moment very fondly, and I cherish the time I spent with her that morning and the memories she shared with me. It was very moving to witness her emotion as she heard Churchill's voice in the Museum's interactive displays." Joanne Grenier-Morton notes, too, that the cigar formed part of a larger donation, which included some Churchill speech notes, signed Greek banknotes and some cigar bands. Elizabeth Nel had replaced the band on the cigar she saved from the fire.
2. I am indebted to Joanne Grenier-Morton for her research into the background of the "cigar" and for providing these details.—Editor.

time later she was able to see it again and sadly discovered that it had dried out in the display case and seemed a lot smaller than "My Cigar" had been after sixty years of her special care.

As we parted at the door, my gracious hostess remarked that for a long time she had done nothing to assess her original memories. Recently she had found that, because of failing memory, she had to write out her talks and this made her think more critically of Winston Churchill. She summed up her thoughts by saying: "Winston may have been difficult, impatient and demanding but never impossible. He had a loving heart and that conquers all."

August 2007.

J. Lionel P. Heath
Rotary District 9320
District Governor 2007-8
Port Elizabeth, South Africa

Appendix 1

Recollections by Elizabeth Nel's children

When asked to write some thoughts on how it was to grow up with Mr Churchill's Secretary as our mother, we, Andrea, Deborah and François, put our heads together.

Apart from the dedicated pictures of Mr and Mrs Churchill, which seemed always to have been there, Elizabeth's natural humility, as well as her devotion to her roles as wife and mother, kept her focus on her husband and children. She did take time off around 1958 to write her book and as we grew up, she quite often went out to give "a talk".

The person who answered *"Would I.."* when asked if she would like a position in the secretarial office of the Prime Minister, was the same person who brought us up. Elizabeth took life with both hands and loved to rise to a challenge. The old values of kindness, loyalty, duty, perseverance, sacrifice, consideration of others and thinking things out for ourselves were attributes which were certainly reinforced during her time with Mr Churchill. She sometimes gave us examples of his strength of character by use of anecdotes and incidents and we heard all about Mr Churchill's English as she tried to steer us from a too heavy South African version.

In the early years she occasionally corresponded with him and told him about her family. She got his blessing before publishing her book and he sent her copies of some of his own publications. She kept in touch with members of the Churchill family and with some of her former wartime colleagues.

Elizabeth's trek to the southern tip of the African continent to marry a true South African must have taken a great deal of chutzpah—especially when one has the option to remain comfortably immersed in one's own culture. Coming to wild Africa in the late forties was no tame ordeal for a young lady—that apart from the cultural divide which required bridging! Never afraid to break the mould and fired by her passion for commitment and loyalty, she and our father, Frans, founded our family. The resulting fusion brought for us, as children, the very best of both worlds, especially in our growth through the culturally rich family landscape upon which our lives became etched. We savoured a potpourri of life experiences, the memories of which seem unique. Both of our parents sacrificed much energy in working for the community—both local and national. Elizabeth's drive to support saw her in office as Life Vice President of the National Council of Women. Part of her work led to her involvement with the upliftment of local, impoverished schools and townships in dire need of development programmes. Through all of this, we still hear the echo of her utterance of the famed Churchillian motif—'Never, never, never give in!'

For Deborah, growing up in suburban South Africa along with our mother's background and wartime connections, which popped up regularly, made life adventurous and often challenging. Looking back, though, she wouldn't change it for the world. Deborah can still picture Sarah Churchill many years ago as she arrived at H.F. Verwoerd Airport, Port Elizabeth, to visit us.

As years passed and public interest in Mr Churchill grew, Elizabeth was called on more and more to talk about her wartime experience. She was also often asked to put the record straight when there were those who sought to find flaws in a man who had earned such acclaim. She was always careful to give the absolute truth about her former boss. She held Mr Churchill in the highest esteem and loved telling people about him. Elizabeth estimates that she addressed over a thousand interested groups and organisations in South Africa. She also came to correspond with people from many parts of the world who wanted to know more.

In the latter 1990's, Celia Sandys arranged a tour by the Churchill Society, retracing her grandfather's experience in South Africa as Anglo-Boer War correspondent, his capture, imprisonment and escape. She invited Elizabeth and Frans to join the party. This was one of the highlights of our parents' latter years.

François recalls one of Elizabeth's recent visits to Cape Town on appointment, to address the local Moths Association celebration of 'VE Day—60 Years On'. At the grand age of 88, Mum held her listeners spellbound with the account of her extraordinary experiences, swaying us from tears to peals of laughter as she related her personal reflections on the 'Great Man'. During a second visit, she topped this performance when the Military History Society erupted into an explosive standing ovation at the end of her presentation, where the atmosphere was so tangible that Mr Churchill was right there with us in person!

In 2005 Deborah accompanied Elizabeth to London to attend the opening by Her Majesty the Queen of the Churchill Museum at the Cabinet War Rooms. She recalls watching in awe as Elizabeth handled press conferences and lengthy BBC interviews with ease—and again as she was presented to the Queen, the Duke of Kent and others.

Andrea went with her in 2007 when the museum had won the European Museum of the Year award and when she had been invited to give the first of The Churchill Lecture Series in the museum auditorium. She left her walking stick by the side of the podium and stood and spoke for one and a half hours. Elizabeth ended by giving her most lasting impression of who Mr Churchill was, with the words "he had a loving heart". The audience rose and applauded her.

Elizabeth continues to swell with pride when asked about the five-year stint during which she worked for Mr Churchill. Her desire to tell the story of this time as a message to others catalysed more strongly in later years. We believe that Mr Churchill, in turn, would be most proud of Elizabeth and her life achievements. She has served as a proponent of the moral code that Mr Churchill employed, during the most challenging of times, to urge the British public on to the greatest heights. One of her favourite hymns, 'I Vow to Thee My Country', spells clearly the theme that she inherited and preached. We, as her children, cannot put in words our deepest appreciation for being exposed to such noble character legacy.

In 2007 in Port Elizabeth, surrounded by family (seven grandchildren included) and friends, she celebrated her 90th birthday.

Note

Andrea is married and lives in Johannesburg. She has two children, Angelo and Desiree, and husband Michael has two children, Margaret and James. Deborah also lives in Johannesburg with her three children, Anton, Martine and Anne-Marie. She lost her husband Dieter to cancer. François and Judy live in Cape Town with their two children, Donne and Jonathan. The grandchildren all have close, loving relationships with Elizabeth, who has become a real South African as they all call her *Ouma*.

APPENDIX 2

Elizabeth Nel: Obituary by David Twiston

From the *Daily Telegraph*, 16 November 2007

Elizabeth Nel, who has died aged 90, was the last surviving personal secretary to have worked for Winston Churchill during the Second World War.

At 10.30 one evening in late May 1941 Elizabeth Layton, as she then was, first encountered the prime minister in 10 Downing Street as he paced up and down in his siren suit.

There was no greeting; he disliked new faces. The new shorthand-typist sat down at the specially adapted silent typewriter, and immediately made a mistake when he started to dictate.

Churchill liked his minutes typed in double-spaced lines, but she used single spacing. He exploded. With the words "fool", "mug" and "idiot" ringing in her ears she was ordered from the room.

More ructions followed when she returned a few days later, not least because the prime ministerial lisp made his words even more indistinct when delivered through the inevitable cigar. Moreover, having recently arrived from Canada, Elizabeth Layton displayed woeful ignorance: she had never heard of chrome or of General Auchinleck.

In addition she wrote "perverted" for "perfervid", and described the Air Minister, rather than the Air Ministry, as being in a state of chaos from top to bottom.

Churchill's curses and growls of complaint continued, but Elizabeth Layton never doubted that she worked for a great man who was under the greatest pressure. Even if he kept her up until 4.30am, as he often did, and had a habit of dictating to her from his bed, in cars or aircraft, or while walking in the garden, he was not unaware of the price he exacted, telling her to take no notice of his irritation, and remarking, when he noted her tiredness: "We must go on and on like gunhorses till we drop."

If he had been particularly short with her he would usually say "Goodnight" in a contrite manner. As a result she retained "furious feelings of devotion".

The young Miss Layton recorded her observations in a diary and in long letters to her mother, which formed the basis of *Mr Churchill's Secretary* (1958), a book that was to be mined by his official biographer, Sir Martin Gilbert.

She noted the way Churchill liked his speeches laid out in verse form; his habit of lighting cigars from a candle which then had to be whisked away because he disliked the smell of it being snuffed out; and how he was most irritable when things were going smoothly, yet sweet when the situation looked dark.

The Chiefs of Staff who entered the secretaries' room before meetings were too preoccupied for small talk, but she found ministers more friendly.

Anthony Eden was affable in his velvet smoking jacket; Ernest Bevin reminded her of a steam shovel; Lord Beaverbrook talked with a snarl; and while General Smuts liked the country house atmosphere of Chequers—though not the late hours—the American Secretary of State, Harry Hopkins, complained of the cold. Sitting silently with Churchill when there was no dictation, Elizabeth noted the way the chimes of Big Ben became intermingled with those of the Horse Guards clock in the early hours; and recalled the time that Nellie, the parlourmaid, saw a "German parachutist" on the Admiralty building (it turned out to be Nelson on his column). There was also the morning that Smokey, the cat, bit a prime ministerial toe while Churchill was lying in bed.

When the flying bombs started Miss Layton refused to abandon work for a shelter, and then screwed up the courage to ask to accompany Churchill abroad. The work on these trips was often as hard as ever. "Gee, are you crazy?" asked a guard in the White House who found her going to bed at 4.30am. "All the American girls went home 12 hours ago."

But she was summoned to meet President Roosevelt, who told her: "I think it is time I met you"; and, after being bidden to join a dinner in the Crimea, which ended with toasts, she was astonished when Churchill leapt to his feet to propose another, to "Miss Layton, the only lady present". A Russian general then seized some flowers from a bowl and dumped them, dripping, in her lap as a bouquet.

After being forced to make a one-line speech of thanks, she found herself taken by the general to a room for another toast, and then another, before rescue came in the form of a senior male secretary.

When she came on duty in Downing Street the night before VE Day, Churchill greeted her: "Well, the war's over, you have played your part."

Elizabeth Shakespear Layton was born at Bury St Edmunds, Suffolk, on June 14 1917, the daughter of a First World War veteran who was advised, because of his tuberculosis, to live in South Africa or British Columbia. The family settled at Vernon, BC, where Elizabeth found the resilience she was to need later when she fell into a frozen pond and had to pull herself out as the ice broke around her.

After leaving school she was sent to a secretarial college in London, and worked at its City employment bureau before going home on holiday in the summer of 1939. She had trained in air raid protection work, and eventually obtained a passage back to London. She worked briefly with the Red Cross before being sent to Downing Street.

Elizabeth Layton remained with Churchill during his brief coalition ministry, and wept with him in his room after his defeat in the subsequent general election. She then announced that she was going to marry a South African soldier, Frans Nel, whom she had met in London after his release from prison camp.

Churchill and his wife Clemmie replied that she must have four children and chanted together: "One for Mother, one for Father, one for Accidents and one for Increase."

The young couple settled at Port Elizabeth, in Cape province, and had two daughters and a son. Elizabeth Nel became vice-president of the National Council of Women and was a strong supporter of her local girls' collegiate. She was in regular demand as a speaker about Churchill, but never met him again.

He sent a telegram protesting about her plan to publish a book, but she knew him well enough to take no notice, and he came round when she approached him a second time. Its combination of affection and honesty won round members of the Churchill family.

In the last holiday she and her husband took before Frans's death in 2000, they accompanied Churchill's granddaughter, Celia Sandys, around the Boer War sights for the book she wrote about her grandfather's time in South Africa.

Elizabeth Nel returned to Britain, once dining with Mrs Thatcher at Downing Street and making a pilgrimage to the home of the Old Etonian Battle of Britain pilot Colin Pinckney, with whom she had been in love before he was killed in action.

In 2005 she was the first person to be presented to the Queen at the opening of the Churchill Museum at the Cabinet War Rooms in Whitehall, and she came back earlier this year to make an 80-minute speech without notes (unlike her master) when it was named a European heritage museum.

The new edition of her book, *Winston Churchill by His Personal Secretary* (by Elizabeth Nel, edited by Charles Muller of Diadem Books) was completed shortly before her death on October 30.

978-0-595-46852-2
0-595-46852-7

Printed in Great Britain
by Amazon